Skies Are Not Cloudy All Day

By William H. Cox

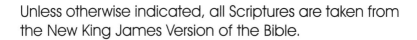

Unless otherwise indicated, all Scriptures are taken from the New King James Version of the Bible.

ISBN 978-1-312-93832-8

Table of Contents

PREFACE

The relationship with God is a curious thing to me. I have always believed in some way that there was someone watching over me. There had to be someone stepping in at just the right time to prevent my ultimate demise. As I get older I do get a little wiser, but I know that it is not so much my doing as it is having my eyes focused on the Lord and hearing His ever so quiet voice saying, *"You probably better not do that."* It took me a lot of pain and many falls to get to this point, and when I finally made the choice to follow Jesus it brought up some questions for me. Initially when He touched me I knew just how real He was, but still wondered, how do I talk to Him and is He really interested in what I think, desire or feel? Why is life always so difficult especially after I've asked Him into my life? I would have thought it would be easier after I accepted His grace. It seems that just when things are going well, something always happens that knocks me back down.

God made us for His pleasure. It is His desire for us to communicate with Him. Because we cannot see Him, it is difficult, but He is very real. When He made us He gave us "free will" to make the decision to have a relationship with Him and gave us a lifetime to make it in. He will not force Himself on you and He waits patiently at the door ready to come in with you, but you need to invite Him in. It says in Revelation 3:20, *"Behold, I stand at the door and knock. If anyone hears My voice and opens the door, I will come in to him and dine with him, and he with Me."*

It isn't always easy walking with God and bad things happen sometimes. When life is good we tend to forget where God is and like a fresh bird dog that gets too far out, we need a little shock to get our eyes back on Him. It stings, but it draws us back in a little closer. Sometimes He uses trials in that same way to draw us to Him or to get our attention. Those trials, when you are going through them, can be painful, stressful and sometimes downright scary. If you turn to the Lord, He is faithful to walk with you. As you go through them together it builds that relationship with Him. It can take a lot of faith for you to take that initial step and reach for Him, and that is why He makes that trial that you are going through so unbearable. Sometimes you have no other choice but to reach out to Him. It may seem cruel at first, but after you get through it you will see where He has taken care of you. I encourage you to reach out to Him and give Him the reins for a while. It is not always the case but I would venture to say that it was probably your own driving that got you where you are today.

It says in Proverbs 3:11-12, *"My son, do not despise the chastening of the LORD, Nor detest His correction, For whom the LORD loves He corrects, Just as a father the son in whom he delights."*

He is our heavenly Father and He loves us. It is mind numbing to me to ponder the depth of His love. The one who created the world, the universe and everything in it, perfectly, wants to walk with you throughout your day, every day. Take a minute and really think about that.

God, our heavenly Father, the One who created the universe and everything in it. He makes the sun come up every morning, makes the seasons change, makes the wind blow, all the way down to making the tiniest little flower bloom for one week out of the year on top of the coldest, rockiest and windiest ridge whether there is anyone there to see it or not. Why? For His glory. Our Father created all of this and He actually loves us and desires for us to communicate with Him. He already knows what we need, want and feel, and yet it brings Him so much joy when we talk to Him and tell him the concerns that we have. You see? By talking to Him it builds up our faith, and in turn that expresses our faith to Him, which gives Him glory. The Bible says in Ephesians 2:8, *"We are saved by faith and not by works so that no man may boast."* That is why prayer and communication with God are so important! God created us for His pleasure, and desires that intimate relationship with us. The more determined we are to seek Him out, the more He will show Himself to us. Start paying close attention. Look for Him; you will see Him at work in your life every day. Watch for His hand in your life and give thanks for every blessing that you see.

I challenge you to try this for a week. Every morning, before you get going, get on your knees for a few minutes and talk to God. Thank Him for everything He has given you and ask Him to show you His hand in your life in some way today. It doesn't need to be a perfectly worded prayer. Just get real with Him. You're not going to pull anything over on Him. He already knows you and your unique personality. He made you that way! Then watch for Him and every time you see Him do something, thank Him and acknowledge it. He will do something unique for you specifically.

If you drive in the car with my friend Bonnie from Colorado, you will hear her say "Thank you Lord" Every time she goes through a green light and doesn't have to stop. She goes through a lot of green lights!

At night before you go to bed write down what, where and how you saw Him. By the end of the week, you will be amazed at how much He does for you and how much you have taken for granted. The more you thank Him, the more you will see Him, hear from Him, and the deeper your relationship with Him will be. Your life will be richer and happier. He loves you and has a plan just for you.

This book is a compilation of experiences that the Lord

has taken me through. It includes the honest communication I have had with Him and some of the lessons that He has taught me through them. It amazes me how He has used various ways to get my attention. It took a little bit for me to figure it out but I look for and rely on those nudges now.

All of the characters are real people and all of the experiences are true. A few names were changed.

As you read this book, take a look back into your own life and reflect on when and where God has done amazing things for you too. Then share them with people that would be encouraged to hear it. Don't keep the good stuff hidden, Go out and Bless Someone!

God Bless You!

Bill

THE TIMING OF AN ANGEL

Merle seemed to sense when I was coming home. He stayed at the ranch while I was gone during fire season. Merle would be busy doing things that dogs do, keeping everything operating on schedule and then suddenly he would run to the edge of the hill and scan the valley below. Cocking his head to one side, he would listen intently for the truck driving through the little town of Peck miles away. When he caught a glimpse of the truck coming up the canyon through the trees, he would turn and race down to the gate located halfway down the driveway. Merle wasn't allowed past the middle gate. Once there he would sit and listen, watching intently for the yellow ¾ ton Ford to come into view.

The driveway was actually more of a glorified cattle trail than a road. One lane, composed mostly of dirt and rock, it contoured the steep hillside for about a mile back to the house. In the spring of the year it wasn't all that unusual to have to stop the truck and kick a few big rocks out of the road to get through. There were two gates on the driveway - one just off the main road, and one halfway to the house. Dad kept both gates closed and locked during hunting season.

I was coming home to the ranch to recover from an injury that had occurred on a prescribed burn. I worked at Priest Lake in North Idaho, just south of the Canadian border, for the Department of Lands. I had pulled a groin muscle loading fire hose and firefighting equipment into a truck. The doctor had given me strict orders not to pick up anything "heavier than a gallon of milk." He suggested not working because there was a risk of a hernia, but had recommended light walking as therapy. To me that was a prescription for elk hunting. My dad was going to be gone on a trip to Montana for business and needed someone to watch the ranch while he was gone, so this worked well for both of us.

When I pulled up to the gate, Merle was waiting patiently. He was an Australian Shepherd / Border Collie cross and was a tri-color meaning that his coat was mottled grey, black and light brown with a white collar. He had two eyes that didn't match. One was bright blue and the other was brown. He had a knob for a tail, and when he was happy his whole butt wiggled. He sat there so obedient waiting for the command to "Load up!" That command was like throwing a switch on a rocket launcher, and he was in the truck sitting as close as possible, butt wiggling and telling me how much he missed me. You couldn't help but laugh at him. That was his greatest desire in life, to be sitting next to me wherever I was. Once the truck started moving again, he was on alert for anything that might need his attention. He kept everything in line at the ranch. Even if no one else noticed, all of the animals knew who was in charge.

The light green house at the ranch was small, cozy and smelled of the country. The roof was metal, and when the giant ponderosa pines that surrounded the place released their long needles you could hear them tap on it. Pine scent drifted down the mountain slope, intermixing with smells associated with ranch life. A hen clucked excitedly as she dove for cover from an amorous rooster, and in the distance a cow bellered for her calf somewhere up on the hill. There was a chain link fence around the house, and a Yamaha four wheeler sat under a low shed next to the barn where the tractor was parked.

I opened the door and walked into the house. The place was cluttered but tidy, with Dad's unique method of organization. There were stacks of magazines opened to specific articles that he planned to read someday when time allowed. Several rifles and a shotgun leaned in the corner next to the sliding glass door. A box of 300 Winchester mag shells and a pair of binoculars were on the far end of the dining room table, next to the cribbage board and three decks of cards. The dishes were washed and in the strainer, long since dried. On top of the refrigerator was a container of syringes and needles, along with a bottle and nipple for feeding calves. A large seven point elk rack was mounted on the far kitchen wall, next to the door to the little bathroom. A lariat draped from the eye guards, along with an old yellow hillbilly hat which hung on another tine higher up.

I looked in the refrigerator and laughed out loud. Dad had made a chocolate pie with graham cracker crumb crust. He knew I loved chocolate pie. "That must be payment for chores," I said. Merle barked when I laughed, and I said, "Okay, I will be right there; just hang on!"

It was chilly in the house. Dad had let the oil stove burn out, since he was going to Montana and wasn't sure when I would get there. I grabbed a napkin, placing it in the stove, and turned the valve on. Heating oil slowly soaked up into the napkin. I lit a stick match from the cardboard box sitting on the shelf, dropped it on the napkin, and closed the door. It would be toasty in the house when I got back. Grabbing a rifle from the corner, I checked to make sure it had shells in the magazine, and headed out to check on the cows. Merle was already on the four wheeler, butt wiggling profusely. He loved the four wheeler. Dad wouldn't let him ride on the back with him, but Merle knew when I grabbed the rifle we were going for a ride, and he was ready to go.

The ranch was about 260 acres of steep hillside infested with yellow star thistle intermixed with mature ponderosa pine trees. It was so steep that if you laid it all flat it would probably be 500 acres. A dirt road wove between eight different fields that hung on the side of the steep hillside. Each field was enclosed with a barbed wire fence to protect the valuable commodity. The cows pastured on the hillsides between them and were turned out into barley fields after the harvest. The only irrigation available was an occasional summer thunderstorm, a gift from God above. Consequently the alfalfa crop depended on the little rain that fell during the summer. In a really good year you might get three cuttings of hay. The house, the barn and the outbuildings sat on a bench overlooking the valley below. A large garden ran parallel to the driveway, with a small greenhouse facing south perched on the edge of the hill for optimum southwest exposure. Every level spot was utilized in some way. The ranch was mostly southwest facing, open with pockets of timber and an occasional apple tree. Heavier brush patches grew around the few springs, with a lone cottonwood marking the water source like a sentinel standing over its treasure. One of the more productive springs fed a cistern that gravity fed to the house, producing sweet cool water.

Merle and I worked our way up the dirt road, past the pond, towards a very steep hill. The road was cut precariously into the side of it, climbing half way up and then switching back on up to the top, where a pocket of ponderosas and a few fir trees towered over the farmland below. The grade was excessively steep, and taking a truck down it in the snow made for a hair raising experience. Upon reaching the bottom, an involuntary sigh of relief was exhaled by everyone in the truck as they resumed normal breathing. The driver would need to shake the blood back into his hands to drive the rest of the way back to the house. When Mother was in the truck the words, "Oh dear!" were repeated multiple times until you reached the bottom, and that was when it wasn't snowing. She refused to ride to the top of the hill when it snowed.

There was an apple tree at the top of the hill that had a little patch of ninebark brush just down from it. The deer liked to bed down in a little pocket there. That evening as Merle and I got close, a huge whitetail buck jumped out and stood broadside. He was about 100 yards away and would be an easy shot. I grabbed the rifle from the rack on the front of the four wheeler and put the crosshairs on him. This was that giant buck that Dad had told me specifically not to shoot. He was a toad! I sat and admired his giant rack. The tines were long, almost 14 inches tall, and I could see that the overall rack was wider than his butt as he proudly walked away. I understood why Dad didn't want to shoot him. Just for the genetics of the deer population alone would be worth it; but I also knew Dad liked seeing this ol' boy once in a while. Several smaller bucks exited the thicket with their white tails swaying back and forth with each bound. They were decent bucks, but I wasn't ready to shoot anything just yet. Merle and I continued on up through the gate and to the back of the long field on top. At the far end was an overlook down into "the hole" where the cows liked to hang out. We sat on the four wheeler glassing the hillsides for deer until it started getting dark before heading back down to the house.

Merle was not allowed in the house, but when he and I were there alone I let him in. He was always on his best behavior when I did.

There was an old avocado green and black plaid couch against a wall between the bathroom and the pellet stove in the kitchen area. My sister, Laurie, and her husband, Dave, had donated it to the cause when Mom and Dad had bought the ranch. It was a late 70's model, a little banged up, weighed a ton but it was clean and comfortable. It folded out into a hide-a-bed. They slept there when they came up from southern Idaho. The whole ranch really livened up when my sisters and the kids came up. With four sisters and their families, there were kids laying everywhere. Those mornings made fond memories. One by one, the kids would wake up and climb up on their parents' laps. At first they were shy and wouldn't talk much, hiding in their parents' arms and wiping the sleep from their eyes. As the smell of strong coffee and Dad cooking breakfast permeated the house they would begin to whisper, then talking and giggling, waking up the next round of little ones. Those were the sweet rewards given to all grandparents. The chore of parenting was over and they were enjoying the fruits of their labor, and Mom and Dad treasured them.

While I was cooking dinner, I watched the local news on the little television in the corner by the sliding glass door. Merle was on the green couch watching my every move. I walked over to listen closer when the weather came on. There was a storm coming in on Thursday afternoon. I told Merle that we should probably take a drive up to Angel Butte and see if we could find us an elk Thursday morning. He wiggled his butt without lifting his head from the couch agreeing wholeheartedly.

Thursday morning we got up early. Tears ran down my face as we drove the four wheeler up to the top of the hill to check on the cows. There was a cold stiff wind blowing that stung my face, and I had to warm my bare hands under my arms before I continued to the end of the field. It felt like snow in the air. I watched several deer cross the field and go over the ridge as it started to get light. The sunrise was brilliant red, a clear indication of the storm to hit later in the day. When we got back to the barn I dropped a round bale in each of the feeders for the heifers with the tractor.

By the time we got all of the chores done it was almost nine o'clock. I made a quick egg sandwich and chased it down with a hot cup of coffee. Grabbing the .270 from the closet, I checked the magazine for shells and headed out to the truck. Dad had given that rifle to me when I was 16. It was a good flat shooting gun. Some people thought it was a little light for elk, but my response to them was that it was all about placement. I had shot several elk and a lot of deer with it. I double checked my backpack to make sure there was an extra box of shells, a couple of knives, a bone saw, rope and anything else I might need. Merle sat in the front seat, keeping an eye on the heifers as we drove down the driveway. We were finally heading to Angel Butte.

My buddy Nick had told me about Angel Butte several years prior to this. Nick was one of my best friends, more like a brother actually. We had gone to high school together and afterward had stayed in touch with each other over the years. Shortly after finishing college and getting married, Nick took a job as the assistant fire warden for the Department of Lands on the Clearwater. He had hunted "The Butte" and seen elk there often; at least, that is what he told me. I had hunted it occasionally but had never seen anything. There were always a lot of tracks, but track soup is pretty bland.

I pulled over when we got on the back roads to unload some coffee. The wind had picked up and the sky was gray. You could feel the anticipation in the air. Getting back in the truck, we wound our way up the gravel mountain road at a pretty good pace. There was a stretch of road where several timbered draws fed into an obscure grassy meadow. This was where Nick had always told me to keep my eyes peeled, so I slowed down, searching above the road for anything that might resemble part of an elk. The meadow below the road was private ground and was fenced with barbed wire. Several times while hunting one of the ridges, I had jumped elk only to hear them crash down the timbered draw and across the road. The twang of the barbed wire fence stretching through the rusty horseshoe nails was like the exclamation point on their escape.

My heart sank when we came around the corner to that coveted stretch of road. A pick-up truck was racing towards us, with a cloud of dust billowing up behind it. I rolled my window up as fast as I could just as it blew past, engulfing us in darkness. Temporarily blinded, I slowed down to let it settle. I was disappointed and looked over at Merle sitting in the front seat.

"Well buddy, no elk today after that knot head blew down the road!"

Merle was looking past me on my side of the road when both of his ears went up. I looked to see what he was looking at, and there through the settling dust was a spike bull elk with a mouth full of grass. I swiftly turned the truck into the ditch, grabbed the rifle off the rack and turned the motor off in one smooth motion. Slowly, I opened the door and as quietly as I could, slipped out of the truck, being ever so careful not to slam the door. I bolted a shell in the chamber and climbed the steep cut bank and side hilled around to the draw where I had seen him. My heart was racing and I was doing my best to control my breathing after climbing the steep bank. The wind was whipping around in all directions and shielded any noise I was making. I expected any moment for the bull to wind me and blow out through the draw, but he just stood there eating grass, looking down the hill to the road below. Without thinking everything through, I pulled the rifle up and squeezed the trigger. The bull didn't know what hit him and piled up where he stood. I walked up to him and that's when reality hit me square in the face.

"Boy, this is a hair bigger than a gallon of milk," I thought. *"How in the world am I going to get him gutted out and in the back of the truck?"* He was the size of a horse. I was standing

there scratching my head when a blue station wagon drove up. This lanky young man got out and climbed up the hill towards me. I thought, *"Oh great, what does this yayhoo want?"* He had a smile on his face and seemed friendly enough. He said, "Hey, it looks like you got yourself an elk! Say, my daughter has never seen one; would you mind if she came up and pet it?"

"Sure, no problem," I said, still trying to figure out how I was going to get this thing in the back of the truck. I had just finished cutting the notches in the elk tag and was attaching it to the hock of the back leg when I looked up and saw this guy carrying his three year old daughter, and walking next to him was a very pregnant young lady. I mean, she was like nine months pregnant! Seriously, any step and she could go into labor! They were all kneeling down petting the bull when I got the courage up to ask. "Uh . . . I kind of have a little problem here," I said, going into the story about how I had gotten a hernia and the doctor told me not to pick up anything more than a gallon of milk. I finished off, saying, "If you give me a hand gutting this thing out and help me get it in the back of the truck, I'll give you half of the elk."

They both looked up at me with wide eyes and then looked at each other, and the pregnant lady just started bawling! *"Oh man! Doggone it! What did I say now?"* I thought. *"Why do I always say the wrong things around women?* You would think after being raised with four sisters I would know what and what not to say!" I am sure my mouth was half open in shock as I stammered, "I am sorry, you don't have to help; I can figure something else out!"

The young man said, "No, we will help you! The reason my wife is crying is because I just got laid off from the mill today. We took a drive because it really freaked us out. We don't know what we are going to do, so we went for a drive in the mountains. We have this little one, and as you can see, another one on the way. We had just finished praying to God to provide for us this winter, when we drove around the corner and saw you up here."

"Well, I don't know about all of that," I said, "but if you can give me a hand, I will cut it up, wrap it, and give half of it to you."

He gutted it swiftly by himself. I could tell he knew what he was doing. She and I held the legs for him. I will say that I felt pretty darn guilty watching her grab hold of the other side of that elk's rack and drag it off the hill. I dropped the tailgate on the truck and backed it into the cut bank. They were able to slide it down the hill and right into the truck. It was the easiest elk I have ever got into a truck! After we got it loaded, I got their contact information, and in no time I was back at the ranch. Once there, I unloaded it with the tractor and hung it in the hay shed. A week or so later Dad and I had it cut and wrapped, and that family had half an elk in their freezer.

I have thought about that day since then and how God used an unsaved, crippled up sinner to fulfill this couple's prayers on Angel Butte. I wonder who the angel actually was that day. It could have gone either way. Think about how perfect the timing was, and how everything fell into place. Even a truck barreling down the road or the dust cloud that engulfed the truck could not interrupt the blessings God had in store for that young couple. Instead He used a cow dog with one blue eye and one brown eye to spot that elk, and relayed it to me to provide for them. When God answers your prayer, nothing Satan throws in the way can disrupt what God has in store for you. He will not only provide meat for the winter, He will have it cut up, double wrapped and delivered to your doorstep! How awesome is that? It just goes to show you how God will use anything He can to accomplish His work. His timing is so perfect, and you can rest in that. He loves you and He will take care of you. I no longer believe in coincidences. When circumstances line up, I take a step back and take a look to see what God is doing, how I am involved in it, and what response He is looking for from me. I would love to hear this young couple's story about how God answered their prayers that day. It still blesses me now when I am waiting on God for prayers of my own. Hopefully, it blesses you as well.

Chew on this:

Can you remember when God used you to bless someone else in a unique way?

Have you ever experienced God's perfect timing in your life?

Has God provided for you in a unique way?

I bet if you look back, there have been times in your life when circumstances and the timing lined up perfectly.

"Look at the birds of the air, for they neither sow nor reap nor gather into barns; yet your heavenly Father feeds them. Are you not of more value than they?" Matthew 6:26

CLOUDY DAYS

I think it was back in the late 80's when my little sister Jenny cornered me. She had an urgency about needing to talk to me. It was springtime. The trees were beginning to green up and the air smelled like fresh cut grass and blooming lilacs. People were out enjoying the warm weather after the long winter: mowing their lawns, going for walks, or basking in the sunshine, like we were on her front porch. She started by telling me about Jesus and how He had died on the cross as the perfect sacrifice for my sins. That it was a free gift from God and if I accepted that gift I could have eternal life with Jesus and our family in heaven. "That's cool," I thought.

She continued and asked me, "Do you want to accept that free gift?"

I said, "Sure, you bet! That sounds awesome!"

She asked me to repeat the sinner's prayer after her, and I did. At that point in my life I figured I was a Christian anyway, so this was really just filling out the paperwork, so to speak. For the most part I had always been a pretty good guy, and nothing really changed after I prayed with Jenny. I mean, most of the time my word was good, I was honest with people, worked hard, and if the clerk at the store paid me too much I always went back in and gave them what they overpaid me. I actually enjoyed helping people out that were down on their luck, with a flat tire or really anything I could help them with. I did drink beer a little too much, probably most of the time, and cussed like a sailor; but shoot, all country boys did that. They still believed in Jesus, heaven, and drinking beer, and would poke you in the nose if you said anything against it - primarily against drinking beer.

I was a lover and not so much of a fighter, and I loved all

the girls everywhere. And I was pretty sure that was even in the Bible, to love your neighbor as yourself or something like that. I believed in the power of the Bible and hid my money in it in hopes that if someone tried to steal the money, God would strike them dead or hunt them down and make them suffer terrible bad. There was a time in the wilderness of Montana when a grizzly came up behind my tent in the middle of the night. I heard him breathing and the snow crunching under his huge paws as he slowly circled the tent. It was not a good situation. It was in the middle of winter and I had all of the food in my tent. Bears were supposed to be hibernating. I held onto the Bible with all my might, hoping it would protect me from that bear. The bear eventually ran off when I yelled at it, so I figured it must have worked. I didn't understand at that time that the power of the Bible isn't in its pages and the cover, but in its author, God Almighty.

Whenever I tried to read the Bible, it never made much sense, and what did make sense made me feel guilty; and frankly, it was just downright depressing. I couldn't figure out what the big deal was with it and yet I felt that I should at least try to read it.

More times than not when I did try, it was late at night after coming home from the bar, too drunk to stand up. I would collapse on the bed, reading with one eye open, because when I opened both my eyes nothing focused right. Nights like that I typically ended up kneeling in front of the toilet puking my guts out. That was when I would really get sincere with God. "Please Lord! Take this away from me and I promise I will never drink again! If not, just kill me, please!" Isn't that the way it is? Whenever we get in a bind or are hurting, we are quick to call on the Lord, but how easily we forget when things get better.

Fast forward several years, and I married this beautiful girl.

Julie was everything I ever dreamed of. She was tall, slender and had a great sense of humor, and she loved to hunt, fish and live in the mountains. I knew the minute I saw her that I was going to marry her. To me, she was pretty close to perfect. We were living the dream, or I thought we were anyway. She had applied for and gotten a job with the Forest Service up the West Fork on the Bitterroot National Forest. We had relocated from central Idaho and moved to this remote little town in southwestern Montana. I think we had been married for around five or six years when my drinking and selfish attitude finally got the better of her.

Time has a way of revealing things that you did not want to see when you were younger. Looking back now I see how my controlling anger, bitterness and the all-around self-centeredness that came from constant drinking had pushed her away. She finally told me to hit the road and I was all too happy to run off in my new found freedom, hitting the bars and chasing women. Life was good! Freedom at last! It didn't take long before my life was spiraling out of control like water flushing down a toilet bowl. But hey, I was still a pretty decent guy. I mean, I was dependable, always to work on time, I worked hard at everything I did and would help anyone who needed a hand. "Can't" wasn't in my vocabulary, and I could do anything I set my mind to doing. I walked away from the divorce with my dog Merle, a cooler, a lawn chair, and a pretty good herd of cows. It took several jobs to make ends meet, but life was pretty dang good.

I kept the mother cows over at a friend's place between Hamilton and Darby. Don liked them there to keep the grass down and because it made it look like there was always someone there, so it worked well for both of us. He and his wife stayed there during the summer, and lived in the more temperate climate of California in the winter. I kept an eye on the place when he was away, and was there often with the cows.

Chew on this:

Have you ever asked Jesus to come into your life?

Did your life change afterwards, or did you continue in the same direction you were going?

Have you ever tried to read the Bible and it just didn't make any sense?

Have you ever promised God that you would follow Him anywhere if He got you out of a bind?

Have you ever thought that the Bible had a special power that could save you from a bad situation or something that could harm you?

Anyone can say that they believe in Jesus, but unless there is a profound change in direction you have reason to be concerned. Because the Bible is the inspired word of God you have to be a born again Christian for the Lord to speak to you from its words. That is why I could not understand the Bible when I tried to read it. That is why they call the Bible the living word of God. The words in the Bible have power to speak to you and have power when you speak the words, but the Bible itself will not protect you. All the power comes from God. If you get in a bind, call on Jesus and He will help you.

God is our refuge and strength, A very present help in trouble.
Psalm 46:1

A DIVINE FALL

It was a hot Friday afternoon, July 1st, 1996. The weekend was going to be a long one with the 4th falling on Monday. When I walked into the Loading Chute in Darby it was "Happy Hour," a little after five o'clock. A volley of, "Hey Bill!" echoed off the walls of the old building as the screen door slammed behind me. There were four guys named Bill that frequented the little western bar and it got downright confusing who was talking to who, especially after a few beers. I had big plans to get some hay in the barn so didn't want to stay long that night. It was always a challenge getting out of there during happy hour, because the minute you sat down you had a beer and two wooden nickels sitting in front of you. The pretty little barmaid would give you a wooden nickel when someone bought you a drink as a placeholder until you were ready for your next drink. I never did like to leave in debt, so in order for me to get out of there quickly I had to slam three beers and buy a round for everyone to be square. This was also how you ended up kneeling in front of the toilet late at night when you didn't get out of there in time.

I arranged picking up the hay with my neighbor, who was sitting at the bar nursing a Coors Light. He had a field of alfalfa close to the house and had just gotten it baled that morning. After finishing up business with him, I bought a round of beers and snuck out the back of the bar.

The hot sunlight hit me full in the face, blinding me for a second as I stepped off the boardwalk. The step was further down than a normal step and it got me every time. The jolt set the alcohol into motion coursing through my veins, causing a warm glow to permeate through my body, making my steps meander dramatically. I had parked the truck on Main Street by the Realty Office, and regained my equilibrium by the time

I got to the sidewalk. Merle heard my footsteps and stood up on the spare tire in the back of the truck. He used the tire as his bed and would curl up inside the wheel to sleep when we were not driving down the road. He used it as his platform to announce to every dog we passed that he was driving by. That dog knew where every other dog lived from Darby, Montana to Pomeroy, Washington and south as far as Boise, Idaho. Everyone in town knew Merle, too. I had worked at the Realty Office before I got divorced, so my truck was always parked on Main Street. Everyone that drove through town saw Merle in the back of the truck. The kids walking home from school all knew Merle, too. One by one, they would all stop by the truck and pet him, and he would gently lick their faces.

On my way to Dan's to check on the irrigation I stopped by the convenience store and grabbed a six pack of Budweiser. I drank two of them by the time I got there. He was out in the yard with a TV antenna in his hand. I asked him what he was up to, and he told me that he needed to get it mounted up on the roof; his wife was coming up for the weekend and he wanted to have this done before she got there. He had a ladder leaning against the house and was planning on climbing up with the antenna in hand and slipping it into the bracket already mounted on the peak. I thought it looked a little scary, since that was also where the power line went into the house and there was a risk of electrical shock. I suggested that I climb the roof. He could hand the antenna to me and then I could slip it into the mounting bracket from the top side, eliminating the risk of shock.

I had put the metal roof on the house for him the previous year and had almost fallen off, so I knew it was steep. I worked my way up and was just about to the peak when I looked down at my feet. I noticed that there was a fine layer of pine pollen on the roof, and wondered if it was slick or not. The next step gave me my answer when my foot went out from under me. I spun around and sat down so I could see where I was going to land. I tried frantically to catch any screw heads with my shoes to slow the momentum, which was gaining by the second. My mind raced through different scenarios to break my fall. I thought of grabbing the top of the ladder when I went by, but did the math in my head and realized that it would probably make my feet swing out at that speed and I would land on my head or back, and that would do more damage than just landing on my feet. I yelled for Dan to get out of the way. If I landed on him it would hurt him. The next thing I knew I was on the ground, and Dan was standing over me.

"That was kind of scary! Are you alright?" he said.

"I think so, but my foot sure hurts. I don't think I can stand up. I really need to get this shoe off!"

When I took off the shoe, my foot was swelling rapidly and turning a pale blue. I said, more to myself and under my breath, "Dang, that's not good."

He took me to the doctor in Darby where they gave me an x-ray. The doctor took one look at it and told me, "You sure did a good job with this one, young man. Your heel is shattered in three places!" I didn't think much of it. I had broken a few bones before; this was no different. He put a cast on it and I called Monica, the gal I was living with at the time, to come and pick me up. She and her two kids had been living with me for several months. We got along for the most part. There were days, though.

Monica went to church on Sundays at the First Baptist church in Hamilton. I went with her occasionally and had gone to Bible study with her a couple of times, too. At church, they talked a lot about Jesus, but for the most part it didn't make much sense to me. It seemed that whenever I tried to read the Bible it was confusing, sober or not.

After about three weeks of me getting strung out on pain medication and alcohol, Monica had enough and she moved out, leaving me to fend for myself in the big house. It was so quiet that it was unbearable.

My dad had always drilled it into my head that "can't" wasn't in my vocabulary. Now it seemed that it was the only thing I could say. I couldn't stand up long enough to cook. Couldn't do chores. Couldn't work, and worst of all couldn't afford to buy beer. My world was tumbling down around me. I felt sorry for myself and let anyone know that would listen. Friends quit coming over. They were sick of listening to it, and of driving me to the store to buy beer. I was kind of freaking out. I didn't have insurance and didn't know how I was going to pay for the doctor bills, let alone the house payment and electric bill that came due every month. I was miserable.

July 28, 1996, I was kneeling on the light blue shag carpet in the middle of the living room in Darby. My face was buried in my hands. Pain shot through my foot with every heartbeat and pain medication wasn't helping. I was crying, not so much from the pain, but from the loneliness and utter frustration of my situation. My life was hopeless. I didn't know what to do.

"Jesus, I have heard about you . . . I need help."

I didn't say what I needed help with. I knew and He knew. I jumped when I felt a hand on my shoulder and felt a surge of power that ran through my entire body. Immediately, I turned and looked at the clock to my left on the entertainment center. The segmented digital numbers brightly displayed 4:28 a.m.

I said, "WOW! Thanks!"

Immediately, something was different. My foot still hurt, but there was this refreshing hope. Hope and the realization that Jesus, the Son of God, had just touched me. It was like an adrenaline rush. The only thing I can compare it to is when my sister, Laurie, and I used to ski together in high school. There was a jump that was actually a rock cliff about 25 feet tall. When you went off of it, the height was so intense that it made you suck in serious air, and when you landed at the bottom, it completely engulfed you in a cloud of powder. It was awesome!

I got up and limped back and forth with the crutches under each arm, from the wood cook stove in the kitchen to the sliding glass doors in the living room looking out onto the Sapphire Range. The skyline had begun to lighten up with the rising sun.

What had just happened? It was too wild! Deep down inside I knew that He had cured me from drinking. No doubt. It blew me away that Jesus had just touched me! I couldn't wait to go to the store to specifically look at the beer section to see what effect it would have on me.

I should emphasize here just how much I used to drink. After getting divorced, I drank a half rack (12 beers) every night after stopping by the Loading Chute for several preliminary drinks. On weekends, I started drinking around 8:00 a.m. and drank until I passed out at night, sometimes up to two cases or more of beer.

When I fell off the roof I was working construction for a guy who was involved in the Alcoholics Anonymous program. It worked for him and he had invited me to a few meetings. I read the book, understood the program, and yet always bought a six pack of beer on the way home from the meetings. I just couldn't quit. The thought of quitting scared the hell out of me. I remember wishing that someone would just kidnap me, lock me in a cell and force me to quit. In reality, I would have fought them if they had tried, but inside I knew I had a big problem. I just didn't know how to deal with it and was kind of scared to even try. It actually seemed impossible. I had friends that could have one beer and stop. I wanted so much to be able to do that, too.

Later that day I drove down to the convenience store specifically to look at the beer in the refrigerated coolers. I walked into the store, bought a pack of Marlboros, hobbled back out to the truck and headed down to the Post Office to pick up the mail. I was limping on crutches with the mail in hand when I realized that I forgot to look at the beer in the cooler while I was at the convenience store!

My life changed dramatically after that day. I knew something profound had happened. I had a desire to read the Bible, and when I read it, I understood what it was saying. When I went to church at the First Baptist Church in Hamilton, Pastor Tom and Sharon, the Bible study teacher, actually made sense. It was awesome! There was a thirst to read the Bible all day and God had given me the time to do just that. I would read from morning until dark and read it from front to back several times. It gave me a peace I had never experienced before. I couldn't imagine living without God and His word in my life.

Six weeks later when they cut the cast apart, my ankle was swollen and pale blue. My bare foot tingled when the cool air hit it, and was hyper sensitive to any touch. Standing on it caused pain to shoot around my ankle and made me weak in the knees. The doctor suggested that a cortisone shot might help with some of the pain. I had never experienced a cortisone shot, and when he said it might sting a little, well, that was an understatement! To this day the word "cortisone" makes my legs knock and hands quiver; I get an uncontrollable tic at the edge of my mouth and my forehead breaks out into a cold sweat.

When the doctor stuck the needle deep into my swollen ankle, a stream of blood spurt out in what seemed like slow motion. I watched it shoot through the air and land on the floor as the medicine came out the end of the needle. I thought I was going to go through the ceiling! Intense pain shot from my foot through my body and into my mind. My eyeballs felt like they were going to explode. A series of words came out of my mouth that would make a convict blush and I grabbed the bookshelf behind me. It creaked and the nurse and I both expected it to come down on all of us. When the nurse's eyes met mine, her once pretty blue eyes described perfectly the terror coursing through my body. I could tell she really did not want to be there. Neither did I. Overall, I think it was pretty much a bad experience for everyone in the room.

Afterwards, the doctor asked me to get up and walk down the hall a couple of times. It did feel a little better but it was mostly because he stopped shooting that burning pain into my foot! When he asked how it felt, I said, "Great! Never better!" There was no way he was sticking me with that needle again. In fact, I never wanted to see him again, ever! I think the nurse felt the same way about me, too. The doctor said that my foot would be tender for the next six weeks, and to limit my walking on it to an hour at a time until I built the muscles up around it.

Even after six weeks it was painful to walk on, and I still could not walk across uneven ground at all. Walking down the gentle slope to feed the chickens took forever so I still used the crutches or just drove the truck. Winter was setting in and I knew I needed to get some firewood in. I had a shed full of kindling for the cook stove in the kitchen, and a friend had dropped off a load of rounds that needed to be split. I was very grateful, but it was barely enough wood for the long Montana winter. I went out an hour at a time to split and stack the wood but it was difficult. I was just going to have to get through the winter with what I had. I put the house up for sale and sold the cows. I didn't have much hay and it was too hard to feed them anyway. It would be even harder when the snow came. I read the Bible every day. No one looked at the house.

My little sister, Anna, called in February and told me that she and her husband, Clay, had some work they needed to have done on their place in Boise. They suggested that I come down for a few weeks to help them out. A change of scenery, a warm house and a few home cooked meals were the opportunity that I needed. I worked at my own pace, which was slow. Anna and Clay were both strong Christians and I watched them interact with each other. They had a respect for each other that I had never noticed before.

I began to realize how I had pushed Julie away. I called Julie and told her that I had quit drinking and had been reading the Bible. I showed her where it said that God hated divorce and suggested that maybe we should consider reconciling, and asked her what she thought about that.

She said, "I don't think God is that cruel."

I laughed nervously; that had stung pretty good. I could see how deeply I had hurt her. I told her I was sorry and that I wouldn't bother her again.

Come mid-March, I went back to Montana. It was still winter there. Snow was on the ground and wood was scarce. The house was cold. Loneliness set in. Again. All of my drinking buddies had disappeared. I heard that they thought I had lost it. Found religion or something. That hurt, too.

The cupboards were bare. I had not eaten anything for a day and a half. I was hungry and I got mad at God. I started yelling at Him, saying, "What kind of God are you? Your word says that You take care of the birds of the field, and how much more will You take care of me . . . I am HUNGRY!!!"

I stormed out of the house and drove down to the hamburger joint in town. I was going to get a hamburger and it would be on His shoulders if the check bounced, and I told Him so.

That hamburger tasted so good. But I was still angry with God. Everyone else had let me down and now even He had, too. I didn't want to believe it, and it really hurt that the one person I had put every ounce of my trust in had let me down. I felt completely alone.

On the way back home, I stopped by the Post Office to get the mail. I opened the metal door and there was a letter from my Aunt Mary in Council. That was weird. I wondered what she wanted. It wasn't Christmas or my birthday. She had never sent me a card for either one, anyway. I opened it up, and there was a check for $300 with a note saying, "You have been on my mind a lot lately. I thought this might help you out. Love, Mary."

Tears welled up in my eyes and I said, "Oh, Lord, I am so sorry!"

I kept going to the First Baptist Church in Hamilton, and kept running into Monica there. Each time I saw her it reopened painful wounds. I needed to find another church. One Sunday, I was driving around trying to find another church to go to, when I happened to drive by Calvary Chapel in Hamilton. I parked on the street, debating on going in. The music coming out of the little church was beautiful. I sat outside listening to it break the stillness of the cold, crisp Sunday morning air. I thought, "That must be what it is going to sound like in heaven." At the end of the service, people began coming out. Several people walked past me and Merle sitting in the truck. Everyone was so friendly. It was like a wave of love poured out of that little white church, and I wanted that love.

I decided to go the next weekend. Over the next few weeks, I met a few guys who had similar stories to mine: single men who had pretty much been wrung through the wringer by women, drinking and all around poor choices, and likely a combination of all three. Carl was a retired Merchant Marine captain, and Chuck owned a fly fishing shop where he guided tourists on float trips down the Bitterroot River. Paul was an old hippie-looking dude from California, transplanted to Victor by choice. It was nice to have a couple of friends again. The conversation was better, too. At the bar, everyone talked about life behind them and past memories. These guys talked about what they were going to do. They were living life and had an energy inside that flowed out of them. I wanted that, too! I never thought I would ever say it, but it was actually more fun not drinking, and I didn't have to worry about driving or slurring my speech anymore. I laughed harder and could walk without bumping into anything, and wasn't embarrassed by what I had said the night before. Previously, for as long as I could remember, I had never had a friendship that did not somehow involve drinking. But these people had a potluck every Wednesday night before a small midweek service. I would sit in awe and watch them talk and laugh with no booze. This was so refreshing and fun. This was the life I wanted.

Chew on this:

Think back on your life when something really tragic happened. It may have been an injury, a death, a divorce or maybe you lost a job you really loved. Whatever it was, it put you in a desperate situation.

How did you handle it?

Did you try to fix it yourself or did you ask God for help?

Did you see God working in the midst of it to draw you to Him?

Have you ever thought you might have an addiction problem?

If so, could you admit it to a loved one?

The bottom line is, are you being honest with yourself and those that love you?

Do you ever feel like you have hit bottom and have nowhere to turn?

Do you feel like you have lost everything that ever meant anything to you?

Have you ever asked God to help you with it?

Before you ask, you need to be sincere and honest with yourself and Him. God knows your heart. He knows when you are sincere or bluffing it. If you seek Him with all of your heart He will help you.

God loves you and if you look back at your situation, I would wager that you can see how He showed up just when you needed Him and felt like there was no hope left.

"My son, do not despise the chastening of the LORD, Nor detest His correction, For whom the LORD loves He corrects, Just as a father the son in whom he delights."
Proverbs 3:11-12,

Skies Are Not Cloudy All Day

A CHANGE IN DIRECTION

It was a Sunday in late April. I came home from church and it was spitting snow. Again. I was sick of seeing the bleak landscape and the browns and grays of winter. Even the snow was dirty. I was out of wood at home and was down to hobbling around on the hillside above the house to pick up any fallen tree branches. My foot hurt, I was hungry again, the house payment was due the next day and I didn't have a dime. The house was so cold. I curled up in bed with my clothes and jacket on trying to get warm. I held Merle tight against me. It didn't help that I had lost close to 40 pounds. There was not an ounce of fat on me.

My eyes got a little wet as I cried out to the Lord, "I give up. I don't know what to do . . ."

Someone knocked at the door.

"That's annoying. Who in the world would be knocking on my door?" I thought. "I do not want to talk to anyone right now, Lord."

The person knocked again and again. Merle barked. Wiping any resemblance of moisture from my eyes, I got up and went to the back door. The guy looked familiar, but I couldn't place just how I knew him.

"Hi Bill," he said. "I don't know if you remember me; I live up the West Fork?"

"Oh, yeah." Now it clicked; he used to work for Fish and Game. Instinctively, I checked into my memory to see if I had done anything wrong recently. Then I remembered that Charlie, the contractor I had worked for before I got hurt, had bought some rough cut pine from him the last job we had worked on.

How in the world did he remember me, though?

"Bill, I am in a little bit of a bind," he said. "I was wondering if you would be interested in renting out your house to me and my wife."

"What?" I thought, trying to get everything into perspective. I was shocked! *"This is unbelievable!"*

"Uh, sure!" I blurted. "When do you need to move in?"

"Tomorrow," he said.

Surprised, I said, "Okay, I will be out today!"

We got rent squared away, and I told him that the place was listed with a realtor and if anyone gave me an offer, he would have the first option to buy it or he would need to be out in a month. He agreed and left to start moving.

I called my new friend, Carl, from Calvary Chapel. Ironically, we had talked before about me renting out my house and Merle and I moving in with him until I got on my feet. The next day I was at Carl's. He gave me and Merle room and board for all of that summer and into the fall. Carl proved to be a huge blessing and a good friend. There is a book in itself on the excursions that Carl and I endured over those few months!

That spring, a friend offered me a job working on a stone foundation at his remote cabin. I told him that I would be slow but would also greatly appreciate the work. Well, I was slow, and at the end of the day my foot hurt bad, but it felt good to work again. At least I was making a little money. Reality was setting in, however. I would not be able to keep doing what I had done for a living anymore.

Before my fall, wages in Montana were not that great and I wore several different hats to make ends meet. Working for the Forest Service in Fisheries and Wildlife and gathering watershed data for hydrological surveys were some of my favorite jobs. Always being in the mountains and walking in the back country woods were fading from future possibilities, though. Construction work was painful and heights still freaked me out. I had sold real estate for a while but I needed a dependable income. There was ranching, but I needed more money and I didn't think I could give anyone a fair day's work as messed up as I was. I looked to the State of Montana for help. I didn't qualify for food stamps or other assistance because I was buying a house.

The state did have a rehabilitation program, however, to retrain injured people like me, and it would pay a good portion for schooling. Unfortunately, you had to come up with living expenses and I was broke. But the main problem was, what kind of work could I do or did I want to do? I took interest exams and the results just didn't seem to fit me. I asked the Lord to please guide my steps, and wherever I was when the house sold was where I would go to school, just as long as it wasn't in Lewiston or Boise. *(Here is a little advice, don't ever say that to the Lord!)* I went to Billings, Missoula, and Great Falls looking at different options. I finally narrowed it down to moving to Billings for CAD computer training.

A couple of weeks before moving to Billings I went over to Lewiston, Idaho to help my folks. Mom and Dad had sold the ranch and bought a motel there. They wanted to upgrade a few of the units and I needed the money before going to Billings, so I agreed to come over and give them a hand with it.

I worked most of the week installing the vinyl flooring and putting in new shower enclosures. I only had one bathroom left to finish when Dad and I got into an argument about God versus religion, and how he thought that all religions were the same and they all had the same god. He had been drinking and I knew better than to argue with him when he was in that condition. His source for backing his argument was a book called something like 635 A.D. I tried to explain to him that even the title of the book he was using to disprove the Bible, backed how time itself revolved around Jesus and His coming to this earth. Jesus's life and death were a significant event in the history of the world and our entire dating system proved it. B.C stood for Before Christ, and A.D. stood for the Latin phrase anno domini which meant "in the year of our Lord." When Christ lived and died here on earth something really big happened! I could not understand how someone so intelligent, with a doctorate degree, could not comprehend something so simple. Arguing with him was like talking to a fence post sometimes, and honestly, we were both pretty stubborn.

In the end I concluded that arguing with him was a waste of time and I needed to get going back to Montana soon. There was a storm coming and my tires were in bad shape. He still had work for me to do and he thought I needed to check out classes at the local community college. My mind was pretty well made up to head to Billings, and it just got uglier the more we talked. I was starting to back up like a stubborn ol' government mule.

I woke up the next morning, still pretty much annoyed with the previous night's discussion. After eating a quick breakfast, I went out to the unit to finish it. While I was working, I was venting to the Lord, telling Him, *"As soon as I set this last toilet I am loading up and heading to Billings!"* I picked up the toilet, lined it up with the wax ring, and slowly pushed it down to get a good seal when the Lord said to me plain as day, not audibly but spiritually if that makes any sense, *"If you leave now you will miss out on the blessing I have for you."*

"Huh?" I thought. Instantly peace fell over me. Completely perplexed, I just stood there staring down at the toilet. *"Did I just hear that?"* The peace I felt was distinct and instantaneous. I thought about that, too. What could turn my frustration into peace like a light switch?

My thoughts were interrupted when I heard Dad call my

name. "Hey Bill, there's a phone call for you. I think it is your realtor in Montana!"

I limped to the motel office and answered the phone, still rattled from what I had just heard.

It was my realtor and she said, "Hi Bill, I have great news! We have a full price cash offer on the house!" She told me that I didn't need to be there for closing; we could do it all via the fax machine and they wanted to close as quickly as possible.

I stood staring out the window with the phone in my hand. The Lord had just spoken to me for the first time, and then confirmed it with the sale of the house just like I had asked Him to.

"Is there any way that this could be a coincidence?"

I paced back and forth trying to organize my thoughts.

The next day I felt like I needed to go for a drive and think. Merle and I got in the truck and drove along the dike by the river winding through downtown, and ended up by the college. While I was there I thought it might be a good opportunity to see what programs they offered. I parked in a parking lot and it happened to be for the printing and graphics communications department. I was pretty good at drawing illustrations with pen and ink and watercolor painting, and had done a few illustrations for the newspaper in Hamilton to make a little extra money. Computers were becoming the rage and I figured I needed to do something along that line to be competitive. It was a Friday around 2:00 in the afternoon, and the campus was pretty much empty. There were a handful of rigs in the parking lot, so someone had to be around. My work boots echoed with each footstep down the empty hall. I felt out of place, wearing worn jeans with a hole in one knee, a dirty old t-shirt, work boots and an old baseball cap.

I saw a light on in one of the classrooms and peered inside. The walls were lined with computers at workstations, and a long wide table ran down the center of the room with chairs around it. It didn't look like what a graphics classroom should look like to me. I knew absolutely nothing about computers and was contemplating this when a tall, attractive redheaded lady stepped out of her office in the back.

"Can I help you?" she said. Her name was Jayme. As we talked, she explained to me what a degree would entail and what kind of work I could expect to get upon completion.

I expressed my concern that school was pretty much negative cash flow and that I needed to get through the program as quickly as possible and get a job.

She told me that the program could be somewhat flexible and that she could help me set up something tailored to what I needed for a job as a graphic designer. That was what I needed to hear.

The State of Idaho transferred my rehabilitation claim from Montana and got me a part time job working for a graphic designer in town.

Everything fell into place. Perfectly.

Chew on this:

Have you ever made plans to do something and it seemed like every turn you made came up a dead end?

Think back. Have you ever heard God's soft quiet voice?

Did it give you an indescribable sense of peace?

God has a plan for your life. If you allow Him to, through

trust and obedience, He will take you on a journey that is full of blessings in tough times as well as times of rest. It may not be the direction that you want to go at that time, but it will be the best for you in the long run. You just need to be receptive and trust Him with all of your heart. God wants to bless us in unimaginable ways that we cannot even begin to comprehend.

Trust in the Lord with all your heart, and lean not on your own understanding; in all your ways acknowledge Him and He shall direct your paths. Proverbs 3:5-6

FOCUS

Prayers are building blocks that God uses to build our relationship with Him. So what is prayer? Is it a set of perfectly chosen words placed specifically in a certain order to trigger a response from God? I do not think so. Personally, I think that is annoying to God. Prayer is getting real with Him, but keep in mind who you are talking to. He isn't the "big guy upstairs." He is God Almighty. We are talking to the Creator of everything that is in existence. This part is important, so pay attention to this. When we accept His Son, Jesus, as our Lord and accept that free gift of His sacrifice, dying on the cross for our sins, He sends the Holy Spirit to dwell within us, and the Holy Spirit dwelling inside of us intercedes for us with God. That is why before you accept Jesus as your Savior you cannot understand the Bible, but after you accept Christ you can. That is what it means to be *"born again."* My friend Roger calls it "complexually simplistic." It is so incredibly easy and yet so complex. It takes faith to believe He is listening to your prayers, and through that faith He will answer them. The action of prayer builds our faith, and it also strengthens our relationship with God through communication. It is the physical act of communication, or prayer with the Lord, that God desires from us. He is our Father and we are His children.

After graduating from the community college in Lewiston, I tried to get back to Montana to work. Three different times I applied for jobs and got hired on the spot. Each time when I was packing for the move I got a call telling me the position had fallen through or the previous person was coming back to work or something unforeseen had happened and they no longer needed to fill that position. This was very mysterious to me.

In the meantime, a handful of businesses in town needed me to get marketing materials out for them. My phone was ringing off the hook and it was driving me nuts! I couldn't concentrate on finding a job back in Montana. I finally clued in that the Lord wanted me to stay there in Lewiston. Yeah . . . Lewiston. Big sigh. I continued designing for these clients, but the photography they provided was less than adequate for the quality of marketing pieces I wanted to design for them. I borrowed an old Nikon camera from my dad and started shooting the photography myself. They were ecstatic with the results, and this opened up a whole new avenue for my business.

It was early fall, steelhead fishing was on, and my sister Laurie came up with her husband, Dave, to visit. Dave and I were driving up the river and he was telling me about this guy, Leo, in southern Idaho, who used a blimp to take aerial photos. He suggested I go down and meet him.

Dave arranged a meeting, and I went down to Boise to meet with Leo at Idaho Airships and see how he did this type of photography. I was intrigued. I really wanted to get more involved with photography anyway, and saw the potential of using aerial photography with the marketing I was already doing. On the drive back to northern Idaho, I was talking with the Lord, telling Him how much fun this looked. I asked Him about being a photographer, and would He bless me in this move? I threw out a fleece to Him, saying, *"Lord, if You think this is a direction I should pursue, would You please help me get a Pentax medium format camera for under $1,000?"*

I searched everywhere for a Pentax medium format camera, knowing that I would find one any day. I looked online, offline and between lines. I couldn't even find a used one for less than $1,500, let alone one for under a thousand. After a couple of months I gave up looking, and pretty much gave up on going to Boise to shoot aerial photos.

One day, as I was heading over to my folks' house to play cribbage with Dad, I stopped at the end of the driveway to check the mail. It had snowed a skiff, and I noticed a lump under the snow. I kicked it with my boot and saw that it was the local advertising newspaper in a plastic bag. As I picked it up, I thought, *"Wouldn't it be funny if there was a Pentax medium format camera in there?"* Shaking the snow off, I threw it in the back of the truck.

That was a Sunday night. At midnight, I still couldn't sleep. Merle jumped off the bed because I was tossing and turning so much. I was laying on my back staring at the ceiling when I remembered the newspaper. I ran out barefoot and in my boxers to grab it out of the bed of the truck.

Meticulously, I skimmed over the ads, searching for anything that might say Pentax. As I got to the last page my hope was dwindling. I turned the page and it popped out like it was written in giant bold type. **Pentax Medium Format Camera, George's Pawn Shop.** I jumped out of bed and screamed, "Whoooo Hooo!!! Whoop, whoop, whoop!" Merle pretty much thought I had lost it, but celebrated with me, barking. I think he figured we were going on a late night excursion on the four wheeler to rid the neighborhood of those pesky cats.

I didn't sleep the rest of the night. There was no price in the ad, but I just knew the Lord was going to bless me with it. I had a client at the hospital that I did marketing for, and knew she went to work early. I got up and drove down to have breakfast and coffee with her, and to eat up a little time as well. When I walked back out of the hospital it was just beginning to get light. I headed across town toward George's Pawn Shop, then decided to pull off the road and talk to the Lord.

I said, *"Lord, I always seem to get ahead of You and I apologize for that. If that camera is over $1000, I will probably still buy it. But I do want to be within Your will. Lord, if going to Boise and shooting aerial photography is the direction that You want me to go, could You please have the guy behind the counter say the word blimp?"* When I had finished praying, I thought to myself, "Why do you always make it almost impossible for the Lord to bless you?"

The bell over the door rang as I walked into George's Pawn Shop. There was a warm, golden glow from the rising sun's rays flooding into the shop. My eyes scanned the store for where the camera might be and settled on the display case next to the cash register. There were angels singing in the background, and a faint smell of wood smoke drifted from the stove in the corner. The wood was popping and I could feel the heat on that side of my body. I stood staring at the camera in the glass case, when a guy came over and opened up the back. I wondered if he was George.

He gave me his best pawn shop sales pitch. "That's quite a camera there, isn't it? I bet it's had only two rolls of film shot through it, and it comes with both of these lenses - the 35mm that is on it and this extra 75mm. It's all pretty much brand new."

"Two lenses?! No way! That is incredible! And exactly the lenses needed for aerial photography!" I thought to myself, slowly nodding. I was trying very hard not to lose any composure that I might've had left. I felt like my eyeballs were going to fall out of my head when he placed it in my hands. It was heavy. And new. Like brand new! I noticed an electric cord that came off one side of the camera.

I asked George as casually as I could, "So what's this here electrical cord coming out the side?"

"You know, that is funny you should ask! The previous

owner was going to attach it to a blimp and take aerial photos with it!"

I tried really hard to not to fall over. *"REALLY? Did I just hear that right? Did he really just say "blimp?"*

At that point I didn't dare look at George for fear my eyes would reveal all my cards. One look and he would know that I was going to buy this thing no matter what it cost!

I looked over at the other lens and asked ol' George as calmly as I could, "So, how much you want for this outfit?"

When he said $999, I froze up. I mean, I couldn't move. Couldn't talk. Shoot, I couldn't breathe! My mind was racing. I was retracing everything that I had prayed to God about and He, God, had just answered my prayer all the way down to the word *"blimp!"* I was flabbergasted. God, the Creator of gravity itself, had just answered my prayer. And fortunately, gravity was holding me solidly in place! I felt like I would fly away if someone bumped me. My mind was racing. God loved me so much that He had not only given me a Pentax medium format camera, but He also gave me an extra lens. But more than anything, He gave me the *"thumbs up"* to move to Boise to shoot aerial photography. At that moment I knew without any doubt I was in God's perfect will. A huge wave of joy and peace settled over me. There was no better place to be.

George, on the other hand, was doing his best to salvage the sale which appeared to be falling through the cracks.

"You know what? It's Christmas, I'll knock 20% off!"

I blinked back to reality. "Umm, okay," I stammered, digging $800 and some change from my pocket. My hands were trembling and I felt like I was having an out of body experience. I realized that the angelic music in the background was actually coming from the radio, but the one true God had just blessed my socks off, and that was more real than I could have ever imagined.

That is how I ended up moving to the desert land of southwestern Idaho. Little did I know that God had a desert experience waiting for me, and He was using that camera to get me there.

Chew on this:

Have you ever prayed for something specific and had God show up and bless you, word for word what you asked for?

Have you ever prayed for something and you absolutely knew it was going to be answered?

Do you think that maybe you might not be getting any prayers answered is because you are not asking God for something specific?

Then when He answers our prayers, we get so excited and shocked, like we didn't believe He would do it!

Which prayers He answers is a mystery to me. Then there's the time factor. Sometimes He answers our prayers in real time, and other times He answers in His time and it can seem like an eternity. There are also times when the answer is just "No," and although we may not want to hear that, we have to trust that it is the best for us in the bigger picture.

If you, then, being evil, know how to give good gifts to your children, how much more will your Father who is in heaven give good things to those who ask Him!" Matthew 7:11

DOORS OPEN AND CLOSE

Merle was getting so old that his bodily functions began shutting down. He was having a hard time making it outside to do "dog business" and could no longer jump in the back of the truck. It was a difficult decision but the humane thing to do was to put him down.

Before I took him to the vet, I picked him up and set him on the tailgate of his beloved old 3/4 ton Ford. I sat down next to him and explained to him that he was going to have to go to heaven to be with Jesus and that I would be along soon. I told him that there was probably a tree just inside the gates of heaven and when it was time he could meet me there, but in the meantime Jesus probably needed help with all of those sheep up there. I explained to him that in order to get to heaven, he would need to accept the free gift that Jesus gave us when He died for our sins and he needed to believe with all of His heart that Jesus Christ was Lord and no one else. That even though he was a good dog, he was still a sinner and needed that ultimate sacrifice to atone for the sins he had committed like the time he got into the garbage, or all of the late nights chasing cows the wrong direction, stealing the cat's food, and stuff which no one else knew about. I looked into those two crazy eyes and asked him if he understood what I was telling him. He looked back into my eyes and ever so gently moved his head towards my ear and licked the side of my cheek. My eyes filled up with tears and I held him close.

As I drove back to the house from the vet's office, the tears just wouldn't stop. I told the Lord that it wasn't fair that a dog's life didn't last as long as his owner. I never wanted a dog again.

Within a month after Merle died another event shook my

entire world. It was a few weeks after I had moved to southern Idaho. My dad accidentally fell down the stairs, hit his head on the door jamb and then hit the cement floor, dying instantly. That is a phone call that will haunt me the rest of my life. It was really hard for me. Dad and I did a lot together. The girls and Mom did their thing and Dad and I did ours. Not that he and I had a better relationship than they did, it was just different. I still miss him dearly and for so many years there were so many questions that I wanted to ask him, but it was too late. Dad could never tell any of us that he loved us, but showed us through his actions. I think that this was especially hard on my sisters. Little girls need to know that their dad loves them. When you have someone you dearly love, don't hold that from them. Tell them before it is too late and you have missed the opportunity.

Dad spent a lot of time and energy arguing and went out of his way to disprove the Bible. When he was younger he wouldn't talk about Jesus at all. He would just get mad. As he got older he mellowed out some and would at least discuss Jesus, but he was usually working some angle to try to show that it was all just religion. Dad and I talked about it a lot. I do not know if he ever accepted that it is a relationship and not a religion. He saw God talk to me in so many ways that it is hard to think that he couldn't see how real Jesus is.

I have not had to deal with death very much in my life so I am probably not qualified to say much about it. I do know the frustration that I have with my dad's death, because I don't think he had an actual relationship with Jesus. I can think of nothing better than to be able to spend eternity with my dad. Based on what the Bible says I am not so sure that he will be in heaven when I get there, and that makes me sad and a little angry with him. All I can do is hope that somewhere along the way that he had reached out to Jesus in his own unique way. You never know when it is going to be your time to go. That relationship with Jesus Christ is one you cannot afford to put off.

I have a good friend that I met at Montana State University. Dan and I were instant friends. We both loved to fish for trout on the blue ribbon streams that flowed through the Gallatin Valley, and skipped a lot of classes to do just that. Dan had a sister named Carrie. Carrie would go with us on some of these adventures. We were the "Trout Fishing Trio" setting out to conquer the trout streams of Montana. Our excursions were always filled with excitement and adventure. When Dan graduated, he got a job and moved to Alaska. That left me and Carrie by ourselves and we became better friends. Eventually life happened and we each moved on in different directions. She graduated and took a job teaching economics in North Dakota. Over the years we would talk once in a while and Dan always kept me informed of where Carrie was and what she was up to.

One day after I had moved to southern Idaho, Dan called and told me that Carrie wasn't doing very well. She had smoked most of her life and had gotten cancer. He said that she didn't have long to live, only a few days really, and that I should probably call her. He gave me her phone number and I called her that day on the way home from work. When she answered I told her who I was and she remembered me, and still had a glimpse of the sense of humor that I admired about her. Her voice was weak, though, and it was difficult to hear her as she spoke through the raspiness in her throat.

I asked her how she was doing.

She responded with a little bitterness to her tone. "Geez Bill, how do you think I am doing? I am sitting here waiting to die."

"Have you gotten things squared away?" I asked.

"What do you mean?" she said. She seemed a little annoyed by the question.

I said, "Carrie, I know when you were a little girl that you used to sing in the choir at church. You told me that years ago. So I have a pretty good idea that you knew Jesus at one time. Have you got things squared away with Him?" I paused and, hearing nothing, continued. "You know He loves you and wants you to come home to be with Him for eternity, but you have to have things squared away with Him before you can go."

Again I paused and heard nothing. I thought, *"Well, this is my last chance to talk to my friend and I am going for broke here."* I said, "Carrie, I know you probably know this, but the only way that you will get to heaven to be with the Lord is if you ask Him for the forgiveness of your sins and then accept Him as your Savior. I will be in heaven because I have done that and have been born again, but this choice is entirely up to you. I hope to see you in heaven."

I paused and again heard nothing. "Are you there?" I asked. I heard a muffled reply that sounded like she said, "I am tired right now."

I said, "Okay, well I love you, Carrie. I hope I see you again," and hung up.

To be honest, I really didn't know how well that went. It didn't sound like Carrie was receptive to anything that I had said and she even sounded annoyed. I prayed that somehow, some way, the Lord would use something I said to touch her heart because I wanted to see her in heaven when I got there.

A few weeks later my friend Dan called me. His voice cracked a little when he said that Carrie had died. They were very close, and my heart broke for him. Then he said, "What in the world did you tell her?"

It kind of took me by surprise and I said, "Umm, I don't

know, I told her that I loved her and Jesus loved her."

Dan said that after the funeral, the person who was staying with Carrie and had gone to the Mayo Clinic with her had said, "Whatever that Bill guy said to her changed her complete demeanor and she had a smile on her face up until she died!"

I was elated. I knew then without a doubt that she had heard what I said, and in her last days had gotten things right with Jesus. No one else can make you smile like that in the face of death! That is dying with God's grace. If you allow Him to, He will get you through anything that you are going through, no matter how tough it is.

Chew on this:

This life is not easy. We connect with people and animals. It hurts when they leave but the Bible says that the body dies but the soul lives on forever.

The question is, do you want to spend eternity in heaven or hell?

Both are very real. Both take a conscious decision. Simply put, you are on one team or the other. There is no sitting on the fence with this one.

So which side are you on? Choose wisely, this answer has eternal consequences.

Jesus said to him, "I am the way, and the truth, and the life. No one comes to the Father except through Me." John 14:6

Skies Are Not Cloudy All Day

DRIFTING AWAY

After moving to southern Idaho and making a few job related moves, the Lord blessed me with a good position shooting photography and doing graphic design work for a Landscape Architect/Engineering firm. Working and making money soon became "the priority." Having a little more money allowed me to get more involved with women who did not hold to the same principles as I did. I began to drift in their direction, and eventually quit going to church altogether. I was backsliding quickly.

I had moved into a subdivision, trying to blend into the professional lifestyle. The way I survived suburbia was by leaving town on Friday night and not coming back until late Sunday night. I spent a lot of my time traveling all over Idaho taking photos. Without a dog, traveling was easy. Life was going well. One weekend I stayed in town at my house and slept in until 9:00 a.m. It was a beautiful fall morning. The leaves were changing color and you could smell that autumn was in the air. I walked outside to enjoy what was probably the last of the warm mornings to drink a cup of coffee on the front step. I sat down and began to notice a strange sound I had not heard before. It was shrill and made the hair stand up on my neck. I got up and walked to the driveway, listening intently. It was coming from all directions. It sounded like . . . screaming children. Everywhere I turned there were screaming children. Riding their little bikes on the sidewalks, playing in their driveways and on the grass. They were everywhere. They even rode up into my driveway, taunting me with their waves and their cheery smiles!

When did this happen? Had this been going on all along? I had made a little money from an investment prior to the screaming children incident, and saw that it was time to move back to the country and get some distance between the neighbors. I needed some cows for my sanity!

I searched everywhere for a little farm out in the country. Everything was so expensive. In order to buy anything that I could afford I had to use some pretty creative financing. The banks were all too willing to accommodate. After a couple of months, I found a place 45 miles from the office. It needed a little work but being the *"Can't never did anything"* kind of guy that I was, I was up for the challenge.

When I tried to buy the ranch, the Lord tried to tell me to wait and I ignored Him. What I wanted was more important. I had an agenda and I figured that I knew what I was doing. I fought tooth and nail to get it, and eventually He gave me what I called The Rusty Iron Ranch & Cattle Company. A year later the housing market collapsed, my job got cut back and I was down to making a large mortgage payment with 3/4 of my previous income. It was tough to make ends meet and the drive was long and expensive. I tried everything I could to drum up any kind of business at work to get more hours. No one was hiring a graphic designer or a photographer. All of my photographer friends were going out of business. The company I worked for started laying people off, too. Every payday, I figured that I would be the next to be cut. It stressed me out. It made me angry and just wanted to work full time.

Between the slowdown at work and a mysterious occurrence of three back surgeries over a period of three years, my antennae came up, especially when two of the surgeries happened on December 21 of consecutive years. Both involved falling hay stacks, so the third year I stayed away from any hay when December 21 rolled around. I was extra careful feeding any hay for the remainder of the winter too. When irrigation season started that spring I attacked it with the veracity of a 30 year old in a 50 year old body. While loading up the pipe trailer, I heard the all too familiar "pop" in my back and the numbing pain shot down my leg. I finally got the message that the Lord was trying to tell me something. Somewhat of a slow learner, I got back into reading the Bible and started going to church again. The Lord had been strangely silent for many years. I missed the excitement of walking with Him and hearing His voice. I missed knowing that I was in His will. I began to realize just how far I was from Him, and where I needed to be. Like the prodigal son, I headed back to my Father.

For me, the Lord seems to use tough times and pain to call me back to Him. I think it is because I might be a little hard headed. In the book of James, there is a scripture that could pretty much be the theme for the ol' Rusty Iron Ranch & Cattle Company here in southern Idaho. You may have heard of it. It is a curious verse: *My brethren, count it all joy when you fall into various trials, knowing that the testing of your faith produces patience. But let patience have its perfect work, that you may be perfect and complete, lacking nothing. If any of you lacks wisdom, let him ask of God, who gives to all liberally and without reproach, and it will be given to him.* James 1:2-5

Why in the world would you consider it pure joy to go through various trials? The first time I ever read this, it made me do a double take. When you read it all in context, you can understand that these trials will actually benefit you in the long run, even though it isn't any fun while you're going through it.

Well, I knew one thing. I could see that by straying from God, I definitely had lacked wisdom. I needed a fresh new dose of it, and if He was giving it generously then I wanted it, and as much as He would give me. The drive to the office from the farm was 45 minutes. I asked for wisdom every day, and I started dedicating that drive time to the Lord. It was "our time" and I used it to talk to Him and to listen to Him talk to me.

Chew on this:

Are you a slow learner too?

Have you ever felt that chastening from the Lord?

Have you ever drifted so far that God had to get your attention?

Is He doing something dramatic in your life right now?

Do you think He may be trying to get your attention?

Once you have made the decision to have Christ as the centermost part of your life, He will hold you close to Him. It is a supernatural experience where the Holy Spirit comes into your heart and resides there. If you ignore that "quickening of the spirit," Jesus comes looking for you. He will not let you wander very far for too long if you are, in fact, a child of His.

It is comforting to know when He chastens you because, although it is not fun, it confirms that you are His child and there is comfort in that.

For I am persuaded that neither death nor life, nor angels nor principalities nor powers, nor things present nor things to come, nor height nor depth, nor any other created thing, shall be able to separate us from the love of God which is in Christ Jesus our Lord. Romans 8:38-39

COWGIRL

One day a friend of mine from work, Aaron, told me that his wife, Hanna, had found some cow dog pups abandoned in a horse trailer. Hanna worked for a veterinarian in town. One of their clients had found them and brought them into her office. She had called Aaron and asked him if he knew anyone who wanted one. I told Aaron that I didn't want another dog.

Mostly I didn't want to go through that pain again of losing something so close. Dogs have a way of getting into your heart deeper than people do. It's that unconditional love, the kind of love that God has for us. But to have that love taken away was too painful. I wonder if that is what God feels when one of us turns our back on Him? I think so. That is why, when one of His sheep strays, He goes the distance to get it back.

Aaron said, "Just go look at them. You need one anyway. You shouldn't be out there with those cows alone by yourself."

I said I would go and look at them but wasn't going to take one home.

I made a promise to myself that I wouldn't take one unless it came right up to me and it literally chose me personally. We walked into the veterinarian's office and Hanna brought in one little pup. It was the last one. She set the little dog down on the ground in the middle of all of us. It looked up at each of us one at a time and then the little ball of fur's eyes met mine. She stood up on her little stubby legs, walked over to my feet, sat down looking straight into my heart and demanded that I pick her up. I bent over and gently lifted her up and held her to my chest. She got in under my coat and nestled in under my arm. Her puppy breath lingered in my nostrils.

"Geez. Okay. I will try it for the weekend," I thought, but reserved the option to return her if it didn't work out.

It was a long weekend. That dang dog chewed on everything, even on the stereo wires. I don't know how she didn't get shocked! I spanked her most of the weekend. She peed in the house even after I took her outside. I was ready to return her by Saturday night.

Monday morning at the office we had our weekly "Monday morning meeting." I brought her in and asked if anyone wanted her. I handed her to my left and passed her on around. There were approximately 20 people seated around a large conference table in the center of the room. Each one held her and commented on how nice of a dog she was and how I should keep her. I watched her eyes as she went from person to person. Her eyes never left mine. By the time she got halfway around the room I had made my mind up. Cowgirl and I would have to work this out. It seemed like forever before she got back around to me, and when she was in my hands again she buried herself deep down the sleeve of my jacket. I whispered to her that I would never do that to her again.

Like Cowgirl, when we make that initial connection with God He wants us to keep our eyes focused on Him, especially as we go from one trial to the next. When a cow dog meets his master he never forgets who the master is, as we should be towards our Master, Jesus.

That started an amazing relationship with one of the finest dogs I have ever had. Her vocabulary is unbelievable. She is the most tender and gentle dog, and I found out early that you couldn't spank her. She was so tuned in to me, all I ever needed to do was raise my voice and she was at attention! She has been a great addition to Rusty Iron Ranch & Cattle Company. She may be timid with me, but she is all business with the cows. Her herding instincts are phenomenal. It is like she can read my mind. She's always at my side and comes to the office with me every day. Cowgirl would prefer to stay in the truck all day compared to staying home away from me. If it is too hot or too cold I will ask her if she wants to come in the office. There is a kennel under my desk, and if she decides to go inside she knows where it is and beelines for it. She doesn't make a sound all day. She does have an issue with road rage on the way home if people drive too slowly; I am not sure where she got that from!

Chew on this:

Have you ever experienced that unconditional love?

Do you focus your eyes on Jesus no matter what trial you're passing through?

Rest assured that Jesus is going through the trial with you. When you focus your eyes on Him it melts His heart, too. He wants that relationship with you and wants to help you through whatever it is that you are going through, so climb into His sufficient arms. Once you realize that He is walking right next to you your trial seems very small. Go ahead, put your trust in Him.

He shall cover you with His feathers, And under His wings you shall take refuge; Psalm 91:4

THE CONVERSATION

When the economy tanked in 2008, scratching out a living on the farm was a challenge, to say the least. Cell phones had the capability of shooting photos that were good enough to rival hand held cameras. With the digital age, anyone could shoot photography. I asked the Lord for direction daily, only to hear silence. At first I was frustrated. I complained to Him constantly about not having enough work and asked Him what I should do. I started woodworking, building rustic furniture from old barns to make a little extra money.

It was in January, a few years back, when I decided to get really serious about hearing from the Lord. I was going to do a fast for 30 days with juice, and was determined to hear from Him one way or another. I had never really fasted for more than three days so didn't know what to expect. The first couple of days were a little tough, with headaches and intense cramps in weird places like my thighs or in my back and stomach. After that it was much easier and I actually enjoyed it. In fact, the fresh vegetable juice seemed to make me almost euphoric. It gave me a little spring in my step. I could climb over the corral fence without making those grunts and old man noises.

On the tenth day into the fast it was so easy, with no desire for food or juice, that I just drank water. It was amazing! But there was a drawback. I had this infatuation with the cooking channel. I could watch it for hours on the weekend. I had visions of all these great recipes in my mind, but still no revelation from the Lord. Sunday morning worship was awesome and I got so choked up that I couldn't sing, but still nothing from the Lord.

Twenty-one days into the fast I woke up and could tell something was wrong. The digital alarm clock was off. It was terribly cold in the house. Cowgirl was curled up right next to me. I looked outside and all the lights were off as far as I could see. It was 4:30 a.m. when I got up to feed the cows and do chores before going to work. The shower didn't work so I knew the pump wasn't working. It was going to be a long day.

As I walked out of the house the wind hit me square in the face, and my nostrils stuck together when I breathed in. Past memories of Montana came to mind. The thermometer was reading minus ten degrees. The water wasn't running; it was frozen solid at the water trough. I pondered what to do. Should I go to work or should I stay home? There wasn't a lot I could do at home. I had all the cabinet doors and water faucets open, but without power the faucets wouldn't be dripping anyways. There was a propane stove in the house but with the power off the fan wouldn't run. All I could do was hope for the best and head into work. I asked my neighbor, Bob, to call me around eight o'clock if the power didn't come on and I would head back. By then my pipes would be starting to freeze.

Bob called me at 8:00, and the word on the street was that the power would be off until 11:00 or noon. I went home and layered up with long handles topped off with Carhartt coveralls. I had a little propane heater and a couple propane tanks, so I started to work on the freezing pipes. By the time the power came on I could barely move. I hadn't eaten for 21 days. There was nothing in my system to generate any heat and I was starting to shake uncontrollably. I needed to stop the fast. I had made a commitment to make it to 30 days and felt that I had gone back on my word with the Lord. When I heard nothing from Him, I felt like I had let Him down.

A month later I still had not heard anything from God and had given up on hearing anything from Him. Calves started hitting the ground and spring was in full swing. The blackbirds were back singing their sweet, "Konk ker klee" along the canal, meadowlarks were singing in the fields and the rooster pheasants were crowing at any loud noise. Calving time is always a fun time of year filled with excitement and anticipation. It's was like a rancher's Christmas. You don't know what you're getting, whether it be a bull or a heifer or an occasional set of twins. I try to get to the bull calves first thing to put rubber bands on them while they are small. The rubber band stretches around a certain part of the anatomy and makes a bull into a steer. I had one cow that was a little challenging to get close to when she had a calf. She was one of the first calves that I had when I bought the place and I saved her for a replacement cow. A friend of mine, Jayme, took care of the cows for a weekend when this cow was just a calf and had named her Bella. The name fit and stuck.

Bella had needed help with her first calf. She had been in labor over an hour and went down on her side. I went up to her and put my hand on her side. The front feet were coming out and pointed down but were huge. I needed to pull the calf. Bert, my neighbor, was driving by and saw me out in the field. He stopped and asked if he could give me a hand, and I gladly accepted. We got the chains on the front legs of the calf, and he had a couple of handles that hooked into the chains. When Bella pushed, we both pulled as hard as we could. Eventually the calf's head cleared the birthing canal and it slid halfway out. I could see the calf blinking but we needed to work fast. Bella was tired and had given up on pushing. While we waited for her to push again and her calf stopped breathing. We pulled and the calf slid the rest of the way out. It was dead. I breathed in its nose and pressed on its ribs but it was no use. Bella was laying on the ground exhausted and was having a hard time getting up. I made a terrible mistake by throwing her calf in the truck without letting her get up and smell it. She didn't know what happened for sure, but she knew that I had stolen something from her.

I watched her that year and she had a deep love for all of the other calves. You could tell that she wanted to be a mom. Her mother instincts were strong, and she became the babysitter when all of the cows went out to feed. Often when I was irrigating in the pasture she would come up behind me and stare at me. I could tell she was still angry with me over her calf.

Bella had heifer calves up until this particular year, so I never needed to work with any of them. This year she had a bull calf. I tried to get in to try to band it and she came at me full of a mother's fury. I figured it might be better to wait until someone came over, and I could separate her and the calf later.

A couple months passed and the bull calf grew fast. It was pushing a couple hundred pounds and I needed to get him cut. I had sold my calf table when I left Montana so the castrating needed to be done the old fashioned way with a rope and muscle.

One sunny spring day, I was headed home from work early as usual, and was talking to the Lord.

I said, "Lord, we really need to get that bull calf cut, and we need to figure out what You want to do with that cow that aborted her calf last year. Do You want to sell her, make hamburger out of her, or do You want to try to breed her again? I need help catching that heifer to take to the sale, too."

I got home around 4:00 and went in to change from my office clothes into my farm clothes. I looked out the window to the corrals, and that heifer was standing by herself in the corral. That was a little unusual since the rest of the cows were laying out on a gently sloping hillside down from the corrals, chewing their cud and enjoying the sweet, warm afternoon.

I finished getting dressed and went out and shut the gate to the corral, and said, "Thanks Lord, You're awesome!"

I walked back and looked at all of the cows laying on that hillside, and saw that the cow that had lost her calf was laying at the bottom of the slope below the rest of the cows, the furthest cow away from me. I said to the Lord out loud, "So what do You want to do with her? Do You want to sell her or breed her? It's Your call."

I had just gotten those words out of my mouth when she stood up, stretched all the way down to her tail, turned and casually walked through all of the other cows towards me. I opened the gate to the corral and she walked in with the heifer.

I said, "Wow, Lord, thanks! You're so awesome!"

All of the other cows stood up, stretched and walked towards the corral.

The next request wouldn't be as easy, and I said to the Lord, "Well, thank You for helping me out, I appreciate it. You're going to need to bring someone by to give me a hand with the bull calf. We need to get it done soon, though; he is getting pretty big and I don't want to get anyone hurt. But, it is all in Your time. I will follow Your lead."

I turned, and said to Cowgirl, "Let's go change the water!" She spun around and headed for the alfalfa field, nose to the ground, looking for a fresh gopher hole.

Grabbing the first section of hand line and I put it in the valve that was attached to the riser, and went over to turn the water on. There was a lot of commotion up at the corral and Bella was bawling like crazy. Even Cowgirl had heard all of the noise and turned her attention that way.

I said to Cowgirl, "What in the world is going on up there?" and headed up to take a look.

As I walked up towards the corral I couldn't believe my

eyes. Bella's calf had somehow worked his way into the main squeeze chute from the front with his butt toward the head gate. The head gate was closed, but somehow he got in there. I jumped over the corral fence and pushed Bella out. I looked at the bull calf in the chute and there was no way he was getting out.

I scratched my head, laughed and said, "Lord, You are so amazing! Thank You!"

Climbing over the corral, I went to the house to call my neighbor, Bob, to see if he could give me a hand stretching that calf out and cutting him. He said that he had to change a couple more lines of irrigation pipe and would be up in an hour or so.

I went back out and finished changing my water, and thought I would get everything ready for when Bob came over. I grabbed the emasculators, antiseptic and a sharp knife and climbed over the corral fence. The bull calf saw me climbing over the fence, stuck his head through the side bars of the chute, and bucked so hard he flipped over on his back spread eagle!

"Unbelievable!" I said. "Thank You, Lord!"

I put a rope on one of his back legs so I wouldn't get kicked, stretched him out and tied it off. Cut, snip and I was done in two minutes, then got the rope off of him, opened the chute, and he was up out of there, walking a little stiff legged but back at Bella's side.

Later that night, as I was walking out in the back field checking the water in the fading light, I had to wonder if that was what it was like when Adam walked with God in the beginning.

You know, if I would have had three guys helping to catch and separate the heifer and the cow and to cut the bull, it would have taken me longer and all the cows would have been stressed out. The Lord did it all in maybe 20 minutes. I think I smiled for a week about that.

God gives you days like these - little nuggets that are truly treasures that you hold onto throughout your life.

Chew on this:

Have you ever had a one-on-one conversation with the Lord?

Do you ever tell God what you need help with specifically so that He knows what you want Him to help you with?

Are there some things you think are too difficult or mundane for God to help you with?

Have you ever been desperate to get an answer from the Lord?

Have you ever tried to do a fast to get an answer from God?

"Ask, and it will be given to you; seek, and you will find; knock, and it will be opened to you. For everyone who asks receives, and he who seeks finds, and to him who knocks it will be opened." Matthew 7:7-8

TRIALS

Often the Lord uses the trials that life drops on us, to draw us to Him. None of them are easy, and when we are in the midst of them it can be downright painful and depressing.

There have been times in my life that have been lonely. One of those times was when my dad died. He was my best friend in a lot of ways. If I had a problem I could always count on him to talk me through it. He didn't always have the answer, but he could always find a way to laugh about something in the midst of any trial. When he died, it left an empty place in my heart. That emptiness lasted for about a year. Each day it got a little better, but it was a process I had to work through, and eventually there came a time when I had to move on. It made it easier for me to do this when I replaced Dad with my Heavenly Father, although it was frustrating at times because when I needed an answer to a question, it seemed like the line was always busy or no one was ever home. I am confident that even though we sometimes feel unable to connect with God, we can give our problem to Him and He will take it. The problem lies not so much in God not taking it, but in us not giving it to Him completely. This is where faith reveals itself, or sometimes the lack of it. Pastor Jim Halbert, from Crossroads Community Church in Nampa, said it like this once, and I have never forgotten it: If you have a problem that you are giving to the Lord, give it to Him *"hands down."* Turn your palms facing down and give it to the Lord. That way you can't pick it back up. That is so right on the money!

I always seem to pick it back up, even though I try so hard not to. Satan will sneak in at the most inopportune time and bring up a problem that I have already given to the Lord, and get me going all over again. Before you know it, I am going off in my mind about something and having quite the conversation with myself. I can beat myself up pretty good and then realize that I am doing Satan's work for him! When you give a problem to God, leave it there.

My good friends Nick and Lori had a trial where God changed their complete direction. Nick had bought and sold real estate off and on while he worked for the Department of Lands in North Idaho. Eventually, through a lot of hard work and God's blessing, Nick was able to move Lori and all three of their boys into a large home with a multi-million dollar view overlooking Lake Pend Oreille. They were also able to buy a large piece of property nestled in the Selkirk Mountains north of Sandpoint, overlooking the Cabinet Mountain Range in Montana. It was stunning. Nick was selling off lots from it and sending part of the proceeds to Africa for mission work.

In 2008, when everything collapsed, they ended up losing it all. I mean all of it. I will never forget Nick sitting on my couch telling me about it. He looked like someone had sucker punched him in the gut. A lot of family and friends had invested in the property overlooking Montana, and he had lost all of their money along with his. He vowed that if it took the rest of his life, he would somehow pay them back or die trying. When I asked him how much it was, he told me. It was so far out of my reach that I felt like I got sucker punched, too. I wondered to myself, "How in the world is he ever going to do that?" It seemed impossible to me.

One thing Nick said that night I will never forget. "This isn't my deal, this is the Lord's deal. He will guide us where He wants us to go and provide for what He wants us to do. I am just the conduit for Him."

I think Nick barely had enough money for gas and a little food to make it to Nevada. He was helping a friend of his in North Idaho reorganize a business that involved Native American Nations across the U.S. Over the next few months, Nick would call and tell me he was in Montana or California or Arizona. I never knew where he would be next. He would share with me how he would run into so many hurting people, and how he had prayed with them and just showed them the love of Jesus. In the spring of 2014 I went up to North Idaho to visit with him at their new house overlooking the lake. The view was unbelievable. Their business was going crazy. He had hired over 20 people, including his three boys to help out with sales. Things had really turned around for them.

I met with Nick later that year for lunch and asked him how things were going. He said that the business was good, but what was more exciting was that all of their team was committed to sharing the love of Jesus with everyone they came across.

Each week they have a conference call where they share and encourage each other the experiences of the many people they had made contact with that week. God was using them to touch people all over the country, in areas where God needed a faithful person to go. It wasn't easy, but Nick and his team stepped up! This was what God was doing in Nick's life. God took him down to nothing to change the original direction of helping people in Africa to where He needed Nick to go. Then, God brought his finances to a level even higher than they originally were. As we were walking out the door to leave the restaurant he said, "Oh yeah, do you remember all those people I owed that money to? I am down to $5,000 left to pay off!" Sometimes it isn't so much about us, but the direction that the Lord needs us to go in. Next time Nick is buying lunch, though!

We carry these burdens around on our shoulders trying to come up with a solution to fix it, when most of time there is nothing we can do about it anyway. This last summer was a tough one at Rusty Iron Ranch & Cattle Co. Although the Lord blessed me with a healthy crop of calves, and one old cow even had twins, work in town at the office was difficult. There just wasn't enough work and it was showing in my paycheck. Obama Care didn't help either. Each month there was that additional expense, which ate up anything left over to live on. I was flat stressing out. I could feel the knots in my shoulders tensing up. I hated leaving the office at noon. It was humiliating; I wanted to work. The paychecks I received were exactly enough for the house payment, so when I paid my ten percent tithe back to the Lord it didn't leave enough to cover the house payment. I had to wait until the following paycheck in order to make the entire house payment. This creative budgeting was shaking me up. I am responsible with the money the Lord gives me and I understand where that money ultimately comes from, so tithing or giving a portion back to God is a no brainer to me. When money gets this tight, it can mess things up in your head. You start to justify actions that might compromise your walk with God. I think that is exactly why the Lord does it. He wants to know where we stand with Him. Will money, health or any of these other trials shake you from your relationship with Him, or will it make it stronger? Will you choose to lean on Him, or try to do it in your own strength? Developing that relationship with you is His ultimate desire and we do that through trust and faith. Once you wrap your head around this, it makes it easier to do what needs to be done. Hands down! Give it to the Lord. It is His deal. You're just there to do what He needs you to do. You're on assignment for the Lord. He is faithful to provide whatever you need for that assignment.

It was July in Southwest Idaho. Big sigh. It was so darn hot that I was out changing the irrigation water in my boxer shorts, and I didn't care what the neighbors thought. Add the irrigation boots into that scenario and it explained why the neighbors didn't visit much in summer! My hay crop was not doing well at all. I really needed to disc it up and replant, but it was the middle of summer, and I couldn't afford it anyway. My first cutting of hay had been pathetic and produced half as much as normal. I need 26 tons of hay to get through winter and usually get half of that in the first cutting. Typically, it rains in the spring, but this year there had been nothing. I got just over 5 tons of hay in the first cutting. Now I was pouring the water to the field and it was still not growing because it was too darn hot for the grass to grow. The neighbors were already cutting their alfalfa and my second cutting of grass hay was barely high enough to cut.

I came home midafternoon depressed about not having work, and saw that the sprinklers weren't working. Walking out to check on the pump, I could hear it running, but there was no water coming out. I wanted to throw up. Temperatures had been hitting over 105 degrees for more than a week. It was brutal. I hate the heat! My productivity and attitude both drop dramatically when it hits 90 degrees. *"Lord?"* I thought. *"What is going on? I cannot do this right now!"*

I called Gordon's Pump in town to come out and take a look. They pulled the pump, and the diagnosis was that the pump was shot and would cost $4,000 dollars to replace. I didn't have $4,000 but I needed the pump to keep the fields green to feed the cows and make hay for winter. They ordered a pump and overnighted it from Portland but it got lost in transit and didn't show up until a few days later.

Gordon and his crew installed the new pump early in the day and he called and told me that the water was running. I needed to move the irrigation pipe over to the next field before moving the cows into the pasture. The four wheeler had started running rough the previous couple of days, and I hoped it would run long enough to move all of the irrigation pipe. I started it, and it almost made it to the gate, sputtered, backfired and came to a stop. Really? I checked the gas and it was full. Pulled the spark plug and it was working. I tried to start it until the battery was drained. Great! Now before I could move the cows into the field I needed to get the four wheeler and pipe trailer out of it! I figured I could disconnect the four wheeler and hook up the truck to the pipe trailer to get it out of the field. First, I hooked the truck up to the four wheeler with a chain and slowly drug it down to the house. When I got it in the driveway, I stepped out to unhook the chain and the bumper was hanging off the truck by one bracket and dragging on the ground with the other. You're kidding! Now the truck was out of commission. I opened the tailgate on the truck to get pipe connections out of it and the handle broke. No way!

Back in the pasture the pipe trailer needed to move just fifty feet into the next field in order to shut the gate. Searching through the toolbox, I found an extra sparkplug for the four wheeler. While the battery was charging back at the house, I moved eleven of the forty-five foot sections of pipe to the other pasture by hand. Finished with that, I went back to the house to try to start the four wheeler. It started up, and I raced to the pipe trailer to hook it up before the spark plug fouled. When I got off of the four wheeler it died again and wouldn't start. Hooking up the pipe trailer, I examined the situation. Fortunately it was parked on a hill. I had one shot - coast down the hill with the pipe trailer in tow, pop the clutch and hope to jumpstart it. Everything worked as planned, but while I was turning sharp to go back up to the gate Cowgirl fell off of the four wheeler. I slammed on the brakes so I wouldn't run over her, and in the process the four wheeler died. I felt like I could have blown a cork. I bowed my head into my chest and said, "Lord, please," while turning the key, and it started! I gunned it to the top of the field and had gotten everything just inside the gate when it sputtered and died.

The four wheeler had seen better days. Dad had it at the ranch in Peck years ago. He had tried side hilling with it one day over to a spring he was developing. Standing on the foot peg on the uphill side as a counterbalance, he hit a rock and it started to go over. He was six feet in the air when he bailed off. That was quite a jump for a 65 year old man! The four wheeler rolled four or five times before coming to rest against the fence in the field below. We rolled it over and let it sit for a few minutes, and to our amazement it started right up. The racks were bent up a little and the wheels were tilted in slightly and the seat had begun to deteriorate, but it had run fine all these years, and overall it got the job done.

Looking at it, I decided it would be more of an embarrassment to take the old thing in to the shop to get it fixed. I grabbed the shovel, leaving the four wheeler where it had died, and walked over to where the irrigation line was going on top of the hill. Water should have been gushing out of the pipe by this time, but there was barely enough water for Cowgirl to cool off in. I hooked the remaining section up and waited for half an hour to build pressure. Still, there was barely enough to run five heads. The pump wasn't working right.

On the way back to the house, along the bottom of the field, I noticed that there had been a badger out in the pasture. There were holes EVERYWHERE! Big ones. Huge ones that went down three feet into the ground. A five-year-old child could have disappeared in some of them. A cow, a calf or even I could fall in one and break a leg and be out of commission. I sighed and headed back to the house. I wanted to throw up again.

I called Gordon back and he told me that this was a brand new pump they had put in, and there must be another problem. A leak somewhere in the line or a plugged check valve at the well casing. He suggested digging down four feet around the casing to see if there was a check valve at the top of the line. I was beginning to get a little annoyed so the digging went fairly fast. It was hot. Sweat was dripping down my face and into my eyes when I reached the main line that teed into the field. There was no check valve so that wasn't the problem. I walked the irrigation main line again and still found no leaks. I worked my way back up to the top of the hill, and filled a few badger holes on the way back to the house. With every shovel full of dirt I pleaded with the Lord. I didn't know what to do. I felt cornered. The sun was getting low on the horizon.

When I got back to the house I tried to call Gordon. It was late on Friday night and no one answered. I leaned against a fence post in the backyard, exhausted. It cracked and fell over!

"You're kidding!" I said out loud. "Unbelievable!"

I snapped, fell to my knees, and said out loud to the Lord, "What do You want from me? You have my complete attention! You know I will do what You ask me to do. Talk to me so I can understand what You want!"

I searched the sky and consciously listened for any semblance of an answer. The first stars slowly appeared in the night sky. Crickets in the field began their evening chorus and off in the distance a rooster pheasant crowed. Nothing from God. Everything was falling apart and completely out of my control. I was doing everything I knew to do.

"Lord, please help me!" Cowgirl came over, sat down and licked my hand.

At that point I was totally focused on the Lord and was looking in every direction for any indication of a response that might come from Him. I picked up the rotted fence post, propped it back in the hole and went to the house hungry and exhausted, thinking, "I am having a desert experience. What should I do?" The Lord was not answering me in any way. I really wanted to hear His voice. I needed to hear from Him.

The next afternoon, I finally reached Gordon and convinced him that the pump was no good. He said that he had one at the shop that might work. They dropped it in the well the following Monday and it produced even less. I called him again. He told me that it was not the pump, that there was another problem. I told him I was unsatisfied with his work and was not going to pay him $4,000 for a pump that didn't work. The original pump was smaller and worked better than the one he was trying to sell me. I was not mad or losing my temper, just frustrated. He called back in half an hour and said that he would order another pump and be out in a few days.

I had been fasting for three days, hoping to hear something from the Lord. It was 90 degrees at one o'clock in the morning and I had to get up in three and a half hours. I grabbed the Bible off the nightstand next to the bed and it fell open to 1 Peter 5. I skimmed down through the passage, hoping to hear something from the Lord.

1 Peter 5:6-11 said, *"Therefore* ***humble yourselves under the mighty hand of God, that He may exalt you in due time, casting all your care upon Him, for He cares for you.*** *Be sober, be vigilant; because your adversary the devil walks about like a roaring lion, seeking whom he may devour. Resist him, steadfast in the faith, knowing that the same sufferings are experienced by your brotherhood in the world.* ***But may the God of all grace, who called us to His eternal glory by Christ Jesus, after you have suffered a while, perfect, establish, strengthen, and settle you. To Him be the glory and the dominion forever and ever.*** *Amen."*

The words in bold above jumped off the page at me. I reread

them slowly and realized that this was all for my growth, and James 3:5 came to my mind: *"Count it all joy when you fall into various trials . . ."* I knew what I had to do. I realized now that how I handled this situation would determine how long I would be in it. I got on my knees, bowed down over the rustic barn wood chest at the foot of the bed, and put out my hands palms down, giving all of this to the Lord. I told Him that I was not going to worry about this anymore, that He could have it all. I thanked Him for everything that He had provided for me and blessed me with. As I prayed, I felt the weight fall off my shoulders. The knots started releasing. I crawled back into bed and immediately dozed off, sleeping better than I had in a long time. I slept so hard that I was late for work the next day, which was still earlier than when the city boys got there.

The next evening my neighbor Bob came over. I have known Bob since 1989 when we both worked on a fisheries crew on the Payette Ranger District. Located on the South Fork of the Salmon River, our crew consisted of six men and women who worked and stayed at the Krassle work station. We worked four 10-hour days during the week and went back into town on the weekends. The work station had limited electricity provided by a generator if it was needed. When the sun went down it got dark and you hit the sack. In the bunkhouse there were three sets of bunk beds in one room, and then a bed in the kitchen area next to the wood stove. The cook stove and the hot water tank were heated with propane, and there was a small table with four chairs around it for eating. We all took turns cooking separately. When the lights went out some of the guys read books by light from their headlamps. Bob and I talked.

When I bought the ranch I knew my friend Bob lived in the general area, but didn't know that he lived down the road just a mile or so. As it was, it worked out well for both of us. We helped each other with haying and other chores we needed an extra hand on. We did each other's chores when one of us wanted to go hunting and coordinated our trips around each other's schedules.

The day after the Lord gave me that scripture and I turned over my problems to Him, Bob stopped by bringing a couple of popsicles with him. A popsicle on a hot summer evening had grown to be one of the simple pleasures on the Rusty Iron Ranch. We sat on the back porch eating the cold treats which were melting fast in the heat of the evening. Bob was aware of my ongoing situation and I gave him an update on the latest events with the pump, four wheeler, bumper, tailgate, hay and fence post. He sat over in the lawn chair staring out into the field, shaking his head.

After a bit he said, "You know when you first got cut back on your job five years ago, I gave it a year for you to give it up here. This is the worst I think I have ever seen things here on the ranch. You barely have enough hay to get you through winter and this irrigation thing is a huge hit. The last thing you need right now is one of your rigs to go down, and you will be finished. What are you going to do?"

Bob has the gift of letting you know how bad everything is going in your life. I am thankful for that, because by looking at it from someone else's perspective it shows me how good God is and how it has been all Him making ends meet.

"Bob, there is nothing I can do. It is ultimately in God's hands. It is His deal. I can only do with what He provides me. I just have to pay attention to what He is doing and follow His lead. I know one thing though, I am not going to sit around and worry or complain about it anymore."

Sometimes for me, when I talk out loud, the Lord speaks to me out of my own mouth. I just need to listen to what He says.

I got to thinking after Bob left that night about what I said to him. I thought about the Israelites being in the desert with Moses. They were there 40 years wandering around. Their downfall was that they complained about everything, although God was with them every day. They could see the cloud by day for shade and a fire in the sky at night for light.

He is that real to us, too. We just need to open our eyes. I thought about everything going on and realized that by cutting me back at the office, the Lord was actually giving me free time to work on that new project he had been revealing to me. Things were tight but I wasn't missing any meals!

When I realized what God was doing, I changed everything I was doing. I began to thank Him for the time He was giving me and for all of the trials that I was going through. Every day, I asked Him for His wisdom and for His direction to push me to do what He wanted me to do. I wasn't sure what that was exactly, but I thanked Him for that, too.

Immediately things began to change. Blessings showed up in the most bizarre ways. I had bought an old grain silo and converted it into a undergrade hydroponic greenhouse. Being cut back at the office, I had the extra time to work on that project. I needed solar panels to operate the hydroponics in the greenhouse section of the silo, and out of the blue a restaurant called needing stock photos to hang on the walls. I sold the photos for the same amount that I needed for the solar panels. Instead of complaining to the Lord I started keying in to how God's timing coincided to my needs. It was always perfect and exactly what I needed when I needed it. I stopped worrying about the problems after I gave them to Him, and started instead looking to see how He was going to resolve them. And He always does. Perfectly.

Chew on this:

Are you going through a tough trial right now?

Are you carrying all of that worry on your shoulders, or have you given it over to the Lord?

Do you tend to pick back up the problems you have given to the Lord?

Try it. Get on your knees and hand it all to Him, hands down. Everything. You will feel that weight lifted off and the smile return to your face. When the worry pops back into your mind, give it to the Lord "hands down", and then watch for the creative ways in which He gets you through it.

Therefore humble yourselves under the mighty hands of God, that He may exalt you in due time, casting all of your cares upon Him, for He cares for you. Be sober, be vigilant; because your adversary the devil walks about like a roaring lion, seeking whom he may devour. 1 Peter 5:6-8

NUDGES

Writing this has taken me on a journey of memories and of the different ways God has spoken to me in my life. I got to thinking about how, when, and where God and I have bumped into each other, and how He has given me little nudges along the way to prompt me into the decision to walk with Him. Now I understand that those little nudges were intended to draw me to Him. If you look back at your own life, you can probably recall some, as well. Here is just one of mine.

In the late 70's and early 80's a majority of the jobs I held were seasonal. While most of my co-workers who were laid off chose to collect unemployment, I just couldn't do that. I felt I was capable of working, so I should work if I could. During this part of my life, I lived in Bozeman, Montana. Whenever my job happened to stop due to the harsh winters there, I would grab my backpack and stick out my thumb. I had two good friends that I usually visited, and I would pick up a little work there when I could. Nick lived in North Idaho and Keith lived in Boise.

There was a certain dress code that guaranteed success whenever I hitchhiked. I always dressed nice with clean clothes, wore my cowboy boots, always had a sign that said where I was going and that said "Please," and most importantly, always carried a fishing pole. After all, fishermen may stretch the truth a little, but everyone loves to go fishing. It was a good conversation starter.

Nick and Lori lived in Orofino at the time, and I had hitchhiked over to spend some time with them. Afterwards, I was heading to Boise to see my friend Keith. My dad had planned on making a trip to Bozeman, so I could catch a ride back home with him then.

Hitchhiking down the Clearwater River never took much time, especially when you were holding a fishing pole, and I was at the junction of Hwy 12 and Hwy 95, south of Lewiston, in the time that it took to drive it.

It was mid-morning in late winter. The early morning fog had lifted and the winter sun was breaking through the quickly dissipating clouds. The warmth felt good and I wasn't in a hurry to get anywhere fast. The long, cold winter in Bozeman was still fresh in my mind, and this felt like a retreat to the Bahamas. I had brought a book with me on this trip, in the event I got stuck somewhere and couldn't get a ride. That didn't happen often and today I just wanted to sit, absorb the sun for a while, and read a good book. The scenery was beautiful; bare cottonwoods and contrasting red willows shadowed the shores along the Clearwater River. A bald eagle flew down river, stirring the geese into an unrestrained frenzy as it passed overhead. Their obnoxious warnings permeated the air over the rushing water of the river. A carpet of green grass escorted the highway on both sides. I was upstream from the mill in Lewiston and the wind was in my favor, so the odor which was the trademark of Lewiston did not encroach into my section of the road.

Propping my red backpack against the guardrail, I chose a reflective stake to sit down and lean against. Letting out a big sigh, I opened the book and began to read. I had gotten through the first page when I heard a car approaching. Not looking up, I stuck my thumb in the air as it passed. The car blew past me, showering me in road dust and small pebbles. *"That was kind of annoying,"* I thought as I continued to read.

I looked up when I heard the tires squeal as the little sports car came to a stop in the middle of the highway. I got to my feet when the backup lights flashed and it started weaving unsteadily in my direction. Backing up was not his expertise and he finally gave it up, coming to a stop about 100 feet from me and halfway in the road. The top was down on the car, and I watched a young man jump out with an enormous amount of energy and exclaim, "Praise the Lord!"

I debated grabbing my backpack and running to the safety of the willows along the river, but my feet wouldn't move so I just stood there. I am sure my mouth was agape because all that came out was a halfhearted, "Uh, yeah."

He said, "You're a Christian, aren't you?"

"Sure," I stammered, "I guess."

He said, "I could tell that you were, I could see the aura around you! Where are you headed?"

"Aura? Really? Uh, Boise," I said, trying to get a grasp at just how far out there this guy was.

"Jump in, I am heading to Kuna by way of Payette. You're welcome to ride along!"

There wasn't a back seat, so I scooted the seat as far back as it would go and put the backpack between my legs in front of me, and laid the fishing pole along the side by the door.

I had just gotten in and was just about settled when he had the car in gear and, with squealing tires, left the safety of my little section of road. As he hit fourth gear, he cranked the music up and yelled, "Praise the Lord!"

In no time, we were flying down the road with Christian music blaring.

"Another journey," I thought. *"How will this one play out?"*

He tried to talk to me, but I couldn't hear a thing between the music and the wind in my ears. I was thankful when he finally turned the music off and I could hear about half of what he was saying. He explained that he was going to Kuna because he and his wife had separated a while back, and the Lord had told him to go and reconcile with her. "Praise the Lord!" he shouted again.

"Good luck buddy!" I thought. *"She is going to think your cheese has slid off your cracker!"*

The more we talked, the more I kind of liked him. He was probably 30, and seemed like a nice guy. You could tell that he had a heart as big as a house, and he definitely had something going on with the Lord! A world I knew nothing about.

We drove out of Grangeville and headed south towards White Bird Grade. That stretch of the highway had recently been rebuilt, and after several years of road construction it was finally finished. The old grade took an hour to wind up from the Salmon River over White Bird Pass to the Camas Prairie. This new road eliminated the winding road and cut the drive down to 10 minutes but was a long steep grade. During the process, they had made a huge cut into the side of the mountain and it was still a little unstable in spots. Occasionally, there were large rocks in the middle of the road that had rolled off of the cut above.

As we rounded a corner and headed into a straight stretch, I looked over at my new friend. He was grinning ear to ear, with his hair blowing at the edges of his wool cap. When I looked back to the road, I caught movement out of the corner of my eye up above the cut bank. It was a rock, about the size of a basketball, rolling and bouncing down the hill. The trajectory looked as though it was going to roll off the cliff about 100 feet above the road, and come hurtling into our lane, right through the top of the car and into my seat! Everything slipped into slow motion; my left hand grabbed the dash as the rock became airborne. By this time, he had seen it, too, and both of us realized that it was going to land inside our car if someone didn't do something fast! In a split second, he cranked the wheel hard to the left and then back to the right. The little sports car responded quickly, its rear end slid sideways into the oncoming lane of traffic just as the boulder hit the pavement next to my door. He recovered from the slide and turned to me and said, "Praise the Lord!"

I said, "YEAH!" *That was close,* I thought.

We continued on down the road paralleling the Salmon River towards Riggins like nothing had happened.

When we got to Riggins we stopped to get something to eat at a little cafe at the edge of town. He went to the restroom, and I found a booth next to a jukebox in the corner. There were a few locals in the place but for the most part business was slow. Searching the menu, I found a cheeseburger that cost $2.95. We were both pretty much broke and were counting out the change between the two of us when the waitress came up. She looked familiar, and I recognized her from high school. She would have graduated with one of my younger sisters but had dropped out of school and moved up to Riggins with her boyfriend. I ordered a cheeseburger, and asked her if we could get it with an extra plate so we could split it. She asked if we wanted fries, and I looked at the change on the table, and then back up at her, and said probably not. There must have been a look of hunger in my eyes, because when she came back out with our order she also had a huge plate of fries. I looked at her to tell her that we hadn't ordered the fries, and she smiled at me and said, "Don't worry about it."

My traveling companion took a knife, cut the sandwich in half and then bowed his head and gave thanks. It was like he was talking to a dear friend when he prayed. I followed his lead and bowed my head, too. I kind of admired him for taking the time to thank God. It just seemed like the right thing to do, especially after our recent experience.

The weather changed the further south we went. We had pulled the top up before going up the canyon from Riggins to New Meadows. It was raining hard when we got to Payette. He needed to stop in to see his sister before he went on to

Kuna, but said he would drop me off in Meridian, where my friend Keith worked at a service station on Main Street. We pulled up to his sister's house in Payette and half a dozen kids poured out, varying in ages from three to eighteen. They all gave him a hug, and his sister stood in the doorway of an older home watching all the excitement. She had a red and white checkered apron on over a pink flowered dress. Her smile was generous and it brightened her entire face. There was a gentle love that flowed from her. She kissed him on the cheek when we walked into the house. He introduced me and she shook my hand, looked me in the eye, smiling, and leaned over to give me a kiss on the cheek, too. I was surprised, but felt honored.

The smells drifting from the kitchen made me realize just how hungry I was. It was around six o'clock when two of the kids brought dinner to the table. I reminded myself to be polite and only eat a little. There was a big chicken on a plate with mashed potatoes, gravy, homemade rolls and all the fixin's. She told us to sit down and eat. We sat down and she sat down, too, but didn't have a plate in front of her. We all prayed. I looked at her out of the corner of my eye and saw how sincere she was when she prayed, too. Afterwards she told us to eat, and we did. All of it. She and most of the kids sat and watched us eat. It seemed to give her so much pleasure to have us eat and compliment her on how good the food was. I felt bad about leaving after eating such a good meal, but he explained to her that he needed to see his wife. She understood, and we thanked her with hugs. I felt like part of the family when we left.

The closer he got to his destination, the quieter he got. I figured that he must have been getting ready for the reaction from his wife. When we pulled into the service station to drop me off, he insisted on meeting my friend Keith. He got out of the car before I could get the backpack off of me, and was over shaking Keith's hand. I thought I heard him say that "any friend of Bill's is a friend of mine!" I looked at Keith, and he had the same look that I probably had when I first met this guy. My new friend turned and gave me a hug and got in his car.

I said, "Good luck," as he drove off, and thought, *"She better latch on to that guy because he has a good kind of love in him,"* a love that I could not explain.

Chew on this:

Look back on your life and try to remember when God gave you a little nudge. How did you respond?

God gives us nudges in our life, and makes them dramatic and memorable so that we will not forget them.

I hope that this book has touched your heart in a way that gave you a little nudge. If it did, I hope that you come up to me when we are in heaven and you give me a little nudge back!

God bless you and enjoy your journey with Him.

Bill

I have posted photos of some of the places and characters in this book. I encourage you to check out more about Rusty Iron Ranch & Cattle Co. Please post a message if this blessed you on the blog site:
http://www.rustyironranch.blogspot.com/

Acknowledgements

First of all, none of this would be remotely possible without God's inspiration. This book is a testament to His ability to use someone completely unqualified to do an exceptional thing. All the Glory goes to Him.

I would like to thank my niece Sarah for being an invaluable source of optimism. She pushed me through this book so graciously with her positive attitude and genuine belief in what God was trying to accomplish. She stayed up many a late night helping me to pre-edit this as well as introducing me to the technology of writing and proofing on the cloud from two different locations

My sister Jenny for bouncing ideas off of. She has been a great source of optimism as well. Her knowledge of scripture helped immensely when I needed it.

Kelly my editor, helped take my words and turn them into a readable format that the reader could easily comprehend. She was able to do this in a way in which the book never lost its flavor.

Nick and Lori who have been such a great inspiration in my Christian walk. Watching them raise their three boys into fine Christian men has been a pleasure. Their walk through a season when God took them to nothing and brought them back has been such a great witness to His goodness and how much He loves us. God bless Nick for having to hear about this book constantly during the writing process while he had his own business to run.

Roger for his honesty and his ability to say what needed to be said in a way that was easy to swallow. That is a gift my friend.

Bad Bob, when I talk to him, the Lord speaks through me, to me. If my neighbor Bob wasn't here to talk to I would probably miss out on a majority of what the Lord was saying to me.

To Molly, my little girl that I love so much. She inspires me in ways she will never know.

Special Note to Reader:

It is my hope that someone gave this book to you. They obviously love and care for you very much and wanted to give you this gift of encouragement.

As I was writing this book the Lord gave me specific instructions. He told me to give it away, and then present you, the reader, with the option to purchase a book for a friend to give to them. In this way everyone will receive this book as a gift. Please buy a book only if you feel like it would bless someone else. With that said, I ask that when you are done reading this, that you please pass this book on to someone you know that might need encouraging or whose life is a little tough right now.

To purchase a book go to:

For a paperback:
www.rustyironranch.blogspot.com

For an eBook:
http://www.smashwords.com

If you would like to join me in encouraging others with God's love, I would appreciate your support with your prayers or a financial gift. God will surly bless you in return.

Thank You,
Bill

Rusty Iron Ranch | PO Box 577 | Star, Idaho 83669